IT'S ALL IN
THE MIX

IT'S ALL IN
THE MIX

Design Ideas for Living Well

DANN FOLEY

SCHIFFER
PUBLISHING

4880 Lower Valley Road • Atglen, PA 19310

Other Schiffer Books on Related Subjects:
Four Seasons of Entertaining, Shayla Copas, 978-0-7643-5731-2
Modern HomeMaker: Creative Ideas for Stylish Living, Sarah Rose Inch, 978-0-7643-6205-7

Library of Congress Control Number: 2023937575

Cover and design by Molly Shields
Type set in Mrs Eaves OT/Sweet Sans Pro/Miller Text

ISBN: 978-0-7643-6721-2
Printed in China

Published by Schiffer Publishing, Ltd.
4880 Lower Valley Road
Atglen, PA 19310
Phone: (610) 593-1777; Fax: (610) 593-2002
Email: info@schifferbooks.com
Web: www.schifferbooks.com

For our complete selection of fine books on this and related subjects, please visit our website at www.schifferbooks.com. You may also write for a free catalog.

Schiffer Publishing's titles are available at special discounts for bulk purchases for sales promotions or premiums. Special editions, including personalized covers, corporate imprints, and excerpts, can be created in large quantities for special needs. For more information, contact the publisher.

To all of my many clients over many years who have gifted me with their trust, kindness, and the precious gift of creating living, breathing homes for them and their families. It has truly been my honor and pleasure.

Design is more than just the beauty it creates; at its finest, it tells the story of who you are and elevates the experience of living well.

—Dann Foley

CONTENTS

FOREWORD

What I love most about Dann's work and his new book, *It's All in the Mix: Design Ideas for Living Well*, is the incredible enthusiasm, optimism, and energy that it has. Whether at a cocktail party supporting a fellow colleague, a launch of his own product, or working with his clients, Dann approaches everything he does with that same level of enthusiasm, optimism, and energy, and it is both inspiring and infectious.

Dann's designs blend his signature mix of classic and modern elements with a vibrant youthfulness that never feels too serious or stuffy. There's an effervescence in his design work that reflects his personality and a bubbly sophistication that allows his work to feel both classic and "of the moment" at the same time.

Not only does *It's All in the Mix* give tips on how to find your design inspiration and direction, how to avoid making some of the most common mistakes, and how to blend design elements to create your unique aesthetic, but it is also a guide in how to create the life you want to live. If you are curious about the design process, interested in finding ways to zero in on your own aesthetic, or just eager to see the beautiful interiors that Dann creates for his clients, then *It's All in the Mix* is for you.

Dann's how-to guide meets coffee-table book is as delightful as he is. It gives readers a clearer path and approachable understanding of how to create a home that allows them to live better today than they did yesterday. Pull up a chair, grab a coffee (or cocktail), and read on to feed your soul!

—Thom Filicia,
top interior designer,
bestselling author, and
television personality

FOREWORD

What an incredible honor to write a foreword for such a talented soul. As a designer and author myself, I found Dann's candid take on the process to be quite refreshing.

I met my dear friend Dann Foley several years back. We were attending the Interior Design Society's national conference, and he was one of the keynote speakers. To know Dann a day is to feel like you have known him an eternity. He's authentic, warm, funny, and incredibly loyal. I think that's why Dann has been such an inspiring pillar of the industry. He has done what so many of us dream about: create a life filled with beauty, laughter, and undeniable passion.

So, with that said, find a cozy corner, pour a glass of wine, and get ready to relish each page as you learn from the best. Dann Foley takes readers on a tour of the beauty he has created over the years and enables them to take on the challenge of design and view the process in an entirely new light. Each page offers thoughtful advice, stunning photography, and inspiration.

Whether you are a seasoned professional or a homeowner looking for advice, Dann offers each of you a chance to learn from his many years of devotion to his clients. From budgeting to the final layers of a project, he generously shares his tips of the trade, enabling you to take on a design project with practicality and flair!

Get ready to be amazed!

—Shayla Copas,
acclaimed luxury designer,
tastemaker, and author

INTRODUCTION

Home means many things to many people, and we each have our own ideas about what makes a house a home. At the end of the day, though, it's the place where you find meaning.

The most satisfying homes are not about stuff; they're about the stories that people tell through their choices. A home reflects who you are and has a deep connection to what makes you feel happy, safe, proud, and comfortable.

For more than thirty years I have made a career of guiding clients through every aspect of home décor. I don't talk to them about specific design styles (modern, traditional, country, etc.). Instead, I speak to them about feelings, desires, and how those thoughts can be manifested in their lives through the choices they make. I am fond of saying to clients, "I am going to give you exactly what you asked for—but in a way you never dreamed possible." My job is to listen and then to help them remove the blinders of a narrow vision, to show them just how clearly those desires can be presented in the way they live.

The number one question I am asked is "Where do I start?" I often tell people to start at the front door: Sweep your doormat. Then, go inside and make your bed. That may sound flippant, but these two simple tasks can change your life! But let's face it: decorating can be daunting, and knowing where to start is often the hardest part. Many people suffer from what I call "analysis paralysis." When you have too many options to choose from, you may never make a choice. The fear of not doing the "right" thing or not choosing the "right" color or fabric keeps many of us from living our most beautiful, comfortable, and meaningful lives.

Building a home is the same as building a life—it is a work in progress. Decorating isn't brain surgery, and nothing is carved in stone. A creative endeavor needs to be pliable; you need to feel your way around and be open to change. However, it's important to start with a plan. The execution of that plan can take as many phases as your heart and wallet can handle, but without first having a plan, you are doomed to fail. Make a list of priorities. Which room do you want to tackle first? What is the overall feel you are going for? Rather than thinking of style in terms of a theme, be more open and more personal. Ask yourself: What do I love? What is my favorite color? What is my favorite pattern? If you don't have immediate answers to these questions, head to your closet. I find most of these answers in a client's

closet. When I see their personal style, their go-to colors and patterns for their own wardrobe, I have a good jumping-off point.

Avoiding costly mistakes is one of the very best reasons to hire a professional. At the beginning of a project, I tell every client, "I am going to spend every nickel you put on the table, but I am going to spend it wisely." Bad judgment is not the same thing as bad taste. Good taste is relative; it is all in the eye of the beholder. Bad judgment, on the other hand, is easily recognizable. The most successful rooms are what I call "high-low"—a mix of refined and accessible.

Every room should have a "Wow!" piece that grabs your attention. It is often with this major item where you have to spend some money. Then, you can go easy on other items to balance out the budget. Budgeting is a fact of life, and value is always part of the equation. Budgets may vary greatly, but I can tell you that everyone's pocketbook is smaller than their desires. I know with certainty that anyone who has ever said to me, "The price doesn't matter," is only fooling themselves. In fact, I can say with *absolute* certainty that price is always the deciding factor.

Ultimately, every conversation I have about design comes back to "What was your inspiration?" For me, there cannot be a greater inspiration than travel. It calms me, soothes me, recharges my creative batteries, and fuels my wonder. I consider myself a wanderer, not a tourist. That is not to say that I don't see everything I should, but no matter where I might be in the world—Europe, India, China—I like to immerse myself in the life and culture of that place. I want to know the history, the food, and—most importantly—the people. My parents and grandparents instilled in me from a young age that travel enlightens and enriches the soul. As a professional designer, I find inspiration everywhere and every day. Traveling is unique, in that wandering far and wide expands the imagination and appreciation for the world. It reminds us that there is so much more out there than just what is in front of us. Turn that corner, take the unknown path—by doing so, I have found that my life and my work have been enriched by inspiration in its purest form.

While travel allows me to draw inspiration from all around the world, another fundamental influence on my designs has been found much closer to home—in my own living room, in fact. Growing up as a child of my generation, I watched television. Long before I thought of a career in design, I was fascinated with old movies (today we call them classic films). Lousy at sports, I used these great old films as a form of escape. Television was at the center of my world. I found myself drawn to the great films of Hollywood's Golden Era. Watching a film from that period was like being transported to another place and time. Today we have CGI and special effects; back then there were

A silver-leaf paper screen and custom silk upholstery fabrics, coordinated with metallic metal and wood finishes, give this sitting space all the glamour it can exude.

sets and stories. Growing up in suburban Philadelphia, I remember watching black-and-white movies on Saturday afternoons. I was mesmerized by the lifestyles depicted on the screen. I was already being influenced about how to live, even then. I used to sit and sketch some of the spaces and details I saw in those old films. I still do that today when I am looking for inspiration for a client or a product for my own lines. I am not above pausing the television to sketch or trace something right from the screen! Truth be told, life is equal parts fantasy and reality. It is my job to blend the two into a living environment that is authentic to each client.

I often say, "We can live with the past, without living in it." I am a traditionalist at heart, but I have no desire to live in a museum. Like everyone else, I want the latest technology and conveniences. However, it's important to understand where you have come from before you can go forward. Your style choices can be forward-thinking, but I assure you that, at their core, those ideas came from somewhere in the past. A perfect example is the use of animal print fabrics and hides. Many people believe that using leopard, zebra, or other animal hide patterns is a trend—that they go in and out of style. Historically, those exotic animal hides have been used in home décor since the days of the Greeks and Romans. There are few items in décor more classical than that. In fact, they are one of the few design choices that are always stylish and sophisticated. They are both traditional and modern at the same time. It is an item from the past that has been transformed and reborn over and over. Today's animal patterns are printed, faux fur, woven, and even offered in a rainbow of colors. They aren't new or trendy; they are transcendent, iconic.

The world around us moves quickly, and we all want a place of respite and safety. Your home's details can change at your own pace, but do not allow your style to remain stuck in the past. Think about the word "inspiration" for a moment. How does it make you feel? What does it conjure in your mind's eye? For me, it is a sense of euphoria—of knowing that I have connected to a truer understanding of who I am. Not every piece is going to rock your world, but every piece should bring you some level of pleasure or comfort. It is sometimes the mix— the relationship between pieces—that brings me the most satisfaction. It might be a memory of a time or place, or it can be something totally new that speaks to you through the juxtaposition of pieces.

I tell clients, "You don't need to be in love with every piece I show you. Each item, fabric, or lamp is just another piece of the puzzle. It is the finished picture that counts." I don't "match"—I coordinate and curate. The most memorable rooms bring together disparate or contrasting pieces. In the final analysis, it's the story everything tells as a single experience that matters. And here's the other amazing thing: it's totally subjective and personal—it only matters how it makes you feel.

Extend that idea beyond those things you choose for your home. At our firm we go further, consulting on a client's wardrobe, hosted events, and all the facets of their lives that express who they are. I realized early in my career that what my clients were craving was much more than a new room. As we went deeper into the design process, I was being asked questions about fashion, how to set a table, how to use their new spaces in different ways, and how to entertain. The first thing clients want to do when they finish their homes is to host a party to share it with friends and family. So, I was drafted as the party planner. I also have a stake in my projects looking their best for these reveal parties. I didn't want caterers and florists rearranging my carefully designed spaces, so I took over the event—from designing invitations to creating menus, signature cocktails, flowers, custom shirts for the wait staff, and even the outfits worn by my clients. We help tell a complete story with every aspect of their personal style. Like life, living well is a series of daily choices we make. Take design into your everyday experience. Be loose, have fun, dress up, dress down, have friends in, or go out. Life is meant to be lived, and your home is intended to be shared.

In today's homogenized retail environment, where everyone sells basically the same looks and items, it is easy to forget what makes us unique. The retail market tries to tell you what you should have. But there is a big difference between being impressive and truly living well. To live authentically requires effort and takes courage. Being impressive is easy, and it is also a losing proposition because you are always playing keep-up. Our homes are meant to reflect who we are, which is an ever-changing and ever-expanding journey. The effort comes in creating the mix by making choices that feed your soul.

Think of this book as a hybrid—a beautiful coffee-table book for your home that is also a helpful how-to. In it, I will give you tools, tips, tricks, and the inspiration to create the life you want to live. By sharing tried-and-true advice from my more than thirty years of running my own design firm, I hope to inspire you to live better today than you did yesterday. As I love to say, it's all in the mix!

Chapter 1

THE ENTRY

In a former entry of my own, a Palladian-style demilune with a limestone top plays host to Asian porcelain, modern candlestick lamps, and a period carved French mirror.

Treat your front door and entry with the same amount of attention and detail as the rest of your home.

This entry is part of the living room; as such, I needed it to be bright and appealing. The new custom doors with decorative iron grills and custom blue stain were the perfect answer. I added a special detail to the decorative iron; the grills are hinged to make cleaning the glass a breeze.

irst impressions are lasting. Start where it all begins: at your front door. It is the place where people stand while they wait for you to open your home to your guests. What do they see? Do you have a worn doormat? Is your front door dirty or in need of a fresh coat of paint? Are your light fixtures and bulbs clean? Do your flowerpots need tending? These are simple fixes and set the expectation for what lies beyond.

For me, the entry is the first opportunity not only to set the tone but to wow the visitor. A foyer is more than just an entry point and more than just a pass-through to the rest of the house. Like the front door, it is the place where you make that first statement about who you are and how you live.

Above: A traditional Charleston piazza is updated and styled for use beyond a mere entry.

Opposite: A high-rise foyer with no direct natural light is an opportunity to make grand gestures with art, flowers, wallpaper, antique accessories, and architectural details to fill the senses as you are drawn to the view beyond.

Here are some tricks you can use when considering your entry, whether it is big or small. Contemplate every surface as an opportunity to make a statement.

The floor, walls, and stairs. All three are easy places to start—but don't forget the ceiling, trim, and doors too. These are all areas to explore and express creativity and personal style.

Let there be light! The right lighting is paramount in your entry. Say yes to chandeliers, pendants, or can lights and don't forget sconces, art lights, and table and floor lamps.

The right furniture pieces. Create visual interest by combining different periods, styles, and materials. I love stacking old trunks to use as a console. Think outside the box.

The stair runner. Make a luxurious or bold statement on your stairs. Consider animal prints such as leopard and antelope.

Add architectural details. These embellishments can include a new or enlarged baseboard, wainscoting, picture-frame moldings, crown molding, and exposed ceiling beams or coffers.

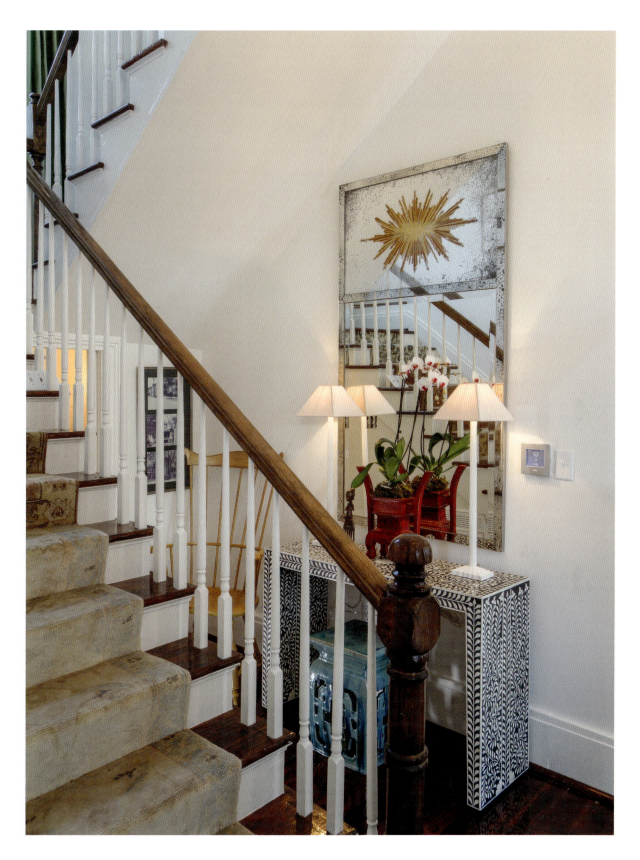

Opposite: I used three different vintage runners to create a unique staircase moment, which is punctuated by the parrot-green silk drapery panels on the landing. Surprise is one of my most important tools of great design.

Above: This stair hall in a historic home needed some punch. The mix of styles, periods, cultures, and materials gives the foyer a real sense of the homeowners' personalities.

I used dramatic and overscaled pieces with memorable details to balance this open entry foyer with the glass doors and lush landscape beyond.

The dramatic scale of the painting, the jade dog, and the tall pedestals overflowing with orchids are balanced by the intricacy of the shagreen on the cabinet and the contrasting colors in the pattern of the rug.

This gallery is an extension of the same entry foyer. More large-scale paintings and pedestals topped with Venetian glass urn lamps lead to an antique stone priest lit by a large skylight from above.

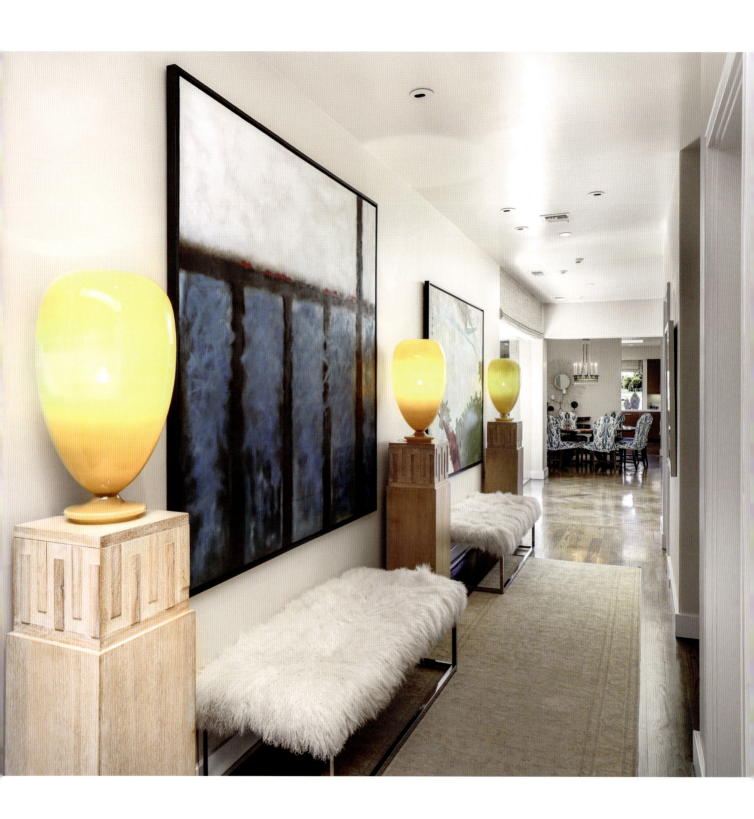

The view from the opposite end of the gallery is just as memorable. The antique runner and the modern hair benches create a pronounced sense of personal style and accentuate the varying proportions of the pieces filling the space.

Left: Even a secondary entry can be treated with aplomb. The high ceiling allowed me to use a hanging fixture on decorative chains. The repetition and the cutouts on the base allow light through to create a strong visual that keeps the space from becoming cavernous.

Right: This gallery hallway links various rooms of the main level. Classic blue-and-white motifs are accented with orange upholstery and florals.

Chapter 2

THE LIVING ROOM

Working with an incredible view such as this
one is like having great artwork; I want
everything to speak to each other, to
enhance one another. One element doesn't
have to overwhelm the other.

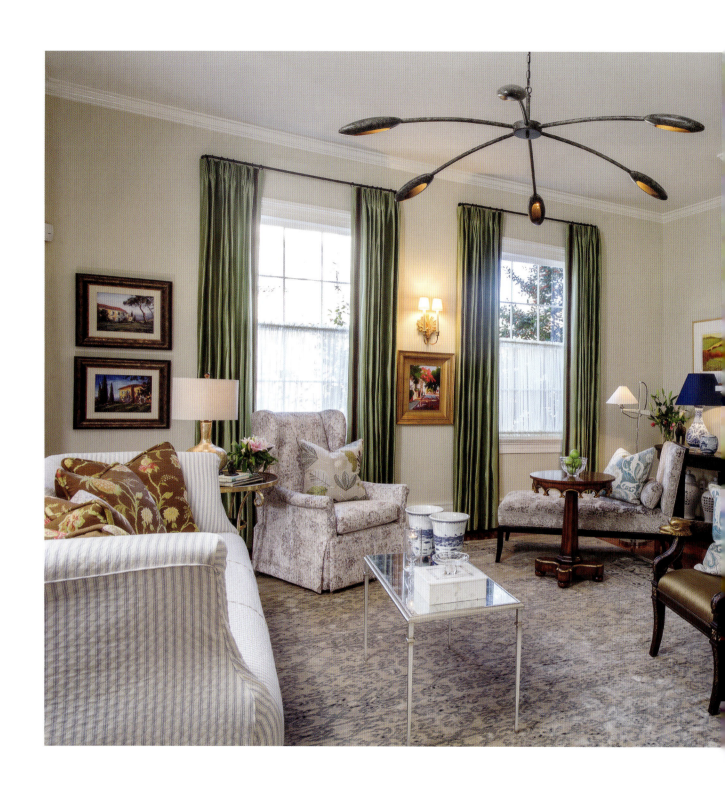

This home on the National Register of Historic Places didn't want to be a museum. We kept and restored all its original details, and I updated the look with a mix of European and American pieces, along with a midcentury modern chandelier to really update the look.

Beautiful is easy.
A living room should be more
than just impressive.
My first priorities are to make
the space comfortable and welcoming.
Living spaces that lack personality
and intimacy are lifeless.

From the opposite side of the room you can enjoy the light from the many windows, all framed in parrot-green silk taffeta.

The original fireplace surround and mantle were restored, and the antique French mirror was added for more period luxuriousness. The custom-made topiaries on the mantle were purposely designed in this lofty height to add both style and drama.

The living or family room gets more use than any other room in your home, except for the kitchen. These two spaces form the foundation for social and family life. In homes blessed with ample square footage, both a living room and a family room make appearances; a living room is usually a bit dressier than a family room. With space at an ever-increasing premium, many homes today forgo dedicated family rooms in favor of the great room, open to the kitchen. This is often a cavernous space that can be quite daunting. The sheer volume can overwhelm furnishings.

A secondary issue is the echo created in this large room, often because of a high ceiling, large windows, appliances in the open kitchen, and the noise of everyday life. Bringing a large room down to a living and intimate scale is the goal. Upholstery, rugs, and window treatments add warmth and beauty to your room—and they have the added value of absorbing sound, which is crucial when you want soothing living spaces or to be able to properly enjoy the sound system on your large-screen TV theater system.

Creating larger gathering spaces for seating with moments of more intimate conversation is key to making a big space feel cozy and inviting. I rarely offer sectional sofas to my clients. In my professional opinion, they do not add more seating, because no one wants to get caught on the inside and be cut off from moving around the all-too-large cocktail table that often goes hand in hand with the sectional. If the room is large, try mixing sofas, love seats, lounges, daybeds, and chairs of varying sizes and shapes to add interest and offer multiple ways of sitting and lounging.

An old house with traditional décor does not have to feel heavy or dated. I chose a softer palette on oversized upholstery for comfort, but I also scaled up and mixed periods with the occasional pieces of furniture to give the space a sense of California traditional style.

Above: A living-room solarium is made even brighter with pale blues, greens, golds, and silver leaf. Leaded-glass doors lead to the indoor pool with limestone decking to match the solarium floor.

Opposite: The scale of the solarium allowed me to use multiple seating groups for smaller gatherings, yet still working together for large groups.

This club room is divided into two areas: one for the TV and bar, and the other for conversation. The warm materials combined with similarly hued fabrics offer a feeling of both comfort and luxury. The final effect, complemented by the unobstructive water views of the room, is that of a vintage yacht. The wood floors are actually the same as on a ship.

The other side of the club room proves that rich neutrals come both in light and dark shades. Fine art can coexist with both color and pattern in a room. They can enliven and enhance each other.

The bar has an extended seating area to
enjoy drinks and TV. Warmth and texture
are the key components of the selections.

The upstairs den of this historic house takes
on a much more casual and working
atmosphere with built-in desks and a
background for the owner's hobbies in
music, guitars, and creating stained glass.

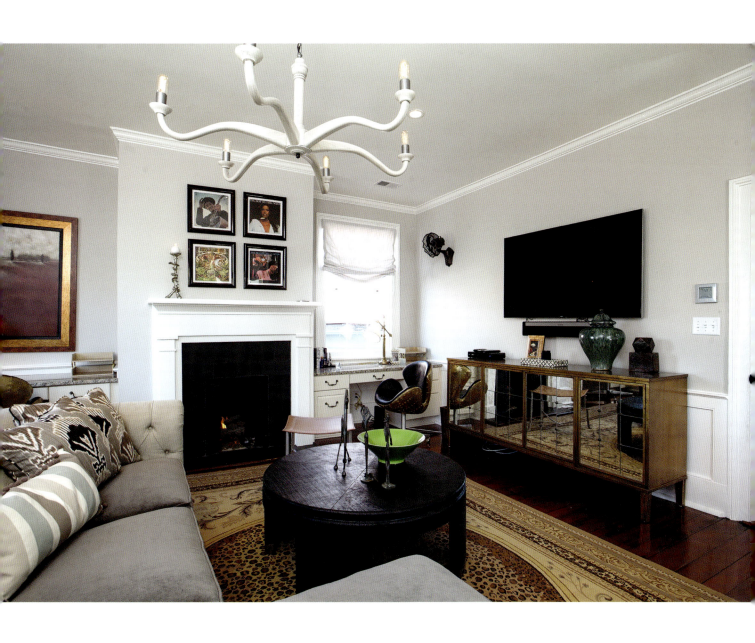

The opposite side of the room is dominated by an antique mirrored and gilded iron console cabinet. The "airstream" vibe of the task chairs and wall fans gives the room a modern vintage feel.

This midcentury high-rise had fantastic views but low ceilings. We countered the latter with a low-profile coffering, which also added much-needed overhead lighting. The ceiling detail has the added effect of visually raising the low ceiling.

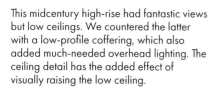

The view from the opposite side of the room offers a glimpse of the foyer and fills the eye with a display of African, Indian, and Indonesian carved art grounded by a gold-leaf panel and a dramatic midcentury-design cabinet, which doubles as a serving bar for entertaining.

The opposite side of the living space offers a more intimate and quiet spot, which enjoys the same spectacular water views. The zinc columns and animal-hide ottoman add contrast to the brightly lit room.

An alcove becomes a high-rise lanai for relaxing with the water view beyond. The iron detail of the sofa creates a modern counterpoint to the exotic art and the vintage French caryatid.

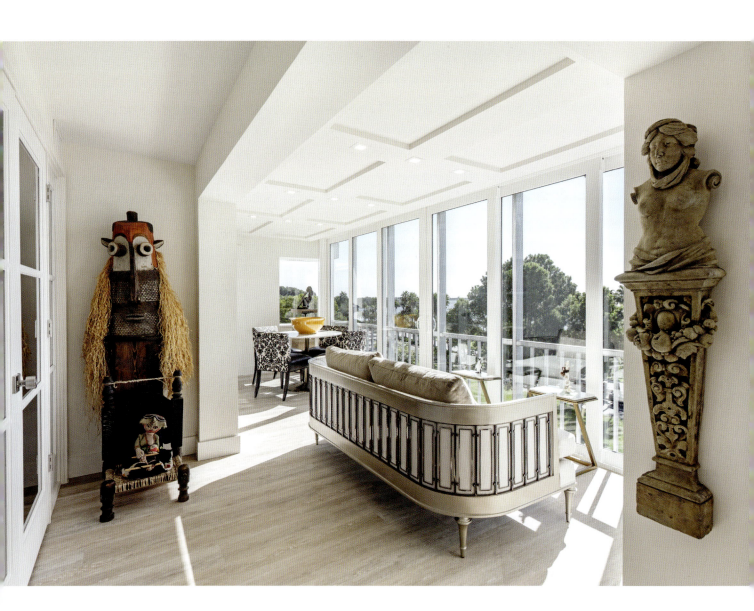

Here are some tips for furnishing and decorating any large room, to create a truly "great room":

A variety of seating makes a room interesting. Including both firm and soft seats, deep seats, and both sit-up and sit-back seating makes a living space comfortable for all.

A sofa with a chaise works better than a sectional. If you face it toward the TV, you will have family and friends fighting over who gets to stretch out on this uber-comfortable choice.

Never underestimate the power of a good lighting plan to create the mood you want to express in your rooms. One way I create intimacy in a large living room is by using a chandelier to bring the volume of the space under control.

Window treatments are key to a finished room. Draperies or curtains can be decorative or operable, and they can be layered with shades and blinds or both, but they are imperative to a beautiful, well-appointed living space.

Let in the light! Many homeowners install blinds and shutters and then never bother to open them. The great news is that many of today's blind and shade manufacturers offer affordable electronic options. You can live like a king by simply pressing a button to open and close your window coverings.

To protect your investment in your home's interior, consider solar shades. I layer them under every treatment and sometimes use them exclusively. Solar shades are made from a type of mesh fabric. The great thing is they can be down and still let the light and view in, while offering privacy during the daytime as well as protection to your interior.

A big cocktail table isn't always better. Keep in mind the scale of the room and the sofa it pairs with. If you choose the ever-popular upholstered ottoman, make sure you have a large tray to provide a sturdy place to sit for drinks, food, and other accessories.

Don't skimp on tables. As a rule of thumb, you will not sit in a chair if you don't have a table within arm's reach to put a glass down. Little tables are like jewelry to a room. They are small but can really sparkle.

Focus the living room for comfort and entertaining. Whether you choose to dress this space up or down is entirely up to you.

This modern great room had to include an open kitchen plan yet still be sophisticated and ready to entertain groups—both large and small.

On the fireplace wall of the same room, I
had custom cabinets and shelves added to
empty niches and floated them over custom
murals of ancient plaster walls. The large
ottoman at the hearth doubles as a pet bed
for the homeowners' dogs.

Arranging furniture is the first step in creating a beautiful room. Your furniture positions should be as unique and interesting as your furniture pieces themselves. Here are some key ways of keeping it interesting:

Don't allow all your furniture to line the walls. Bring some of those pieces into the center; let them float.

Use chairs of every shape, style, and "seat." They are like the mix of people at an interesting party. A room full of different personalities, each standing on their own, with their own voice, is an interesting party and room.

When using area rugs, don't concern yourself with making sure every furniture leg sits squarely on the rug. The rug is not an island—allow furniture pieces to overhang and intersect the lines of the rug and the floor. Layering rugs is always an option too; just be careful not to create a tripping hazard.

When it comes to the relationships between pieces, remember it is all in the mix. Forget about matching suites of furniture. Choose pieces that have character and visual interest, as much as comfort. Curating and contrasting pieces makes a room more memorable and personal.

Mix fabrics too. Mixing patterned and textured fabrics is easy. Scale is the trick; as long as you keep changing up the scale of patterns, they cannot clash. The "fight" that mixing patterns can cause occurs when they are all too similar in scale—not in style. I can fill a room with a variety of plaid fabrics alone if I like, as long as I continue to change up the pattern and scale.

Opposite: As the sun filters into this intimate sunroom, the warm coloring of the columns, beams, and windows creates a rich contrast between the light and dark materials.

Right: A traditional southern living room has a moment of luxurious intimacy in this corner grouping. Luxury should be found in the large and small details, such as the skirt of this banquette paired with the fabrics on the Parisian-style slipper chair.

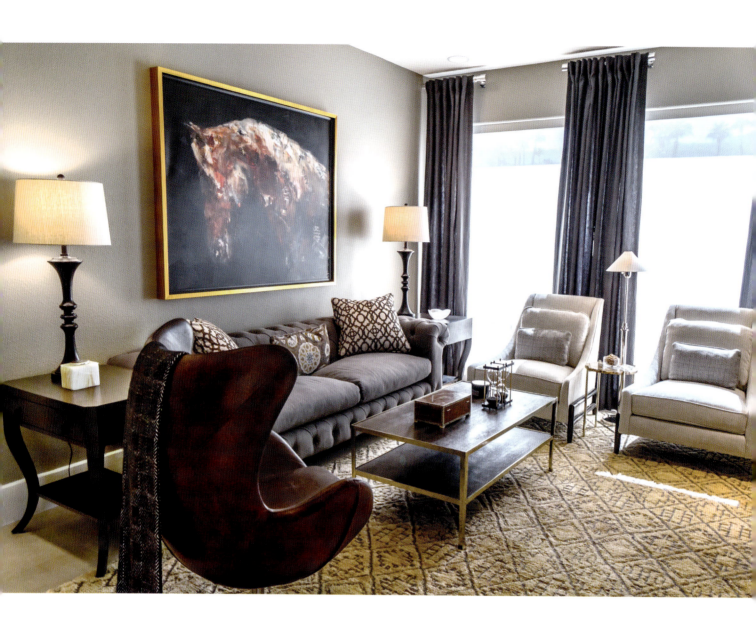

Above: Masculine energy infuses this room through materials, textures, and shapes—but don't mistake this space for some man cave. This room goes beyond gender stereotypes; it is for everyone to enjoy and feel welcome.

Opposite, top: The opposite end of the room is a long view across the dining area toward a new asymmetrical fireplace. The large dual chandeliers define the large room as one space and bring down the volume of the room to a more intimate level.

Opposite, bottom: This living room lacked intimacy due to the volume of the space. Warm neutrals, varied textures, and oversized upholstery created a room that invites you to lounge and relax.

Top: My client requested that the design for this space reflect the feeling of a modern Parisian salon. Silver tones, reflective materials, antiques, and period-style modern pieces are layered in the room to soothe and inspire.

Bottom: This seating area felt exposed since it is bordered by so much glass. The scrim sheer grounds the seating group and diffuses the sunlight yet retains the view. The layered cocktail tables are a combination of an antique Chinese low table and a Parisian-style art deco mirrored table.

The chandelier acts as the center of the
universe in this multi-seating-group living
room. All the furnishings and details seem to
orbit it like the sun.

Mixing silver, gold, antiqued mirror, and
eglomise (reverse painted glass) finishes
gives this room a feeling of richness, and the
space is capped by a starburst chandelier
that is 60 inches in diameter.

All too often I see important architectural details repeated for no other reason than a lack of consideration and imagination. Change it up! I designed this fireplace detail to be in direct contrast to the fireplace detail of the living room. The matte leather finish on the granite and the seaming creates a strong vertical detail and textural moment in this room surrounded by glass.

The floating hearth is grounded by the antique Chinese box, and the large oil painting is dramatically displayed on a standing easel. The contrast of materials and use of black as a repeating accent generate considerable personal style.

This home needed a completely new look and perspective. As if the patio, pool, and views were not already breathtaking enough, our client acquired not one but two important paintings celebrating the desert landscape. The living room needed detail that would not fight the views and art. Quiet colors and patterns, subtle details in materials, and an eglomise cabinet give this room layers of luxury.

The open dining room works more as an anteroom to the living space. In the dining room, I used a darker shade of blue gray on the walls and a hand-painted silk chandelier from Fortuny to give the space its own identity.

I grounded the floating sofa here with a desk and chair, positioned for both form and function. The desk also gives the homeowners the catbird seat to command the home.

Chapter 3

THE DINING ROOM

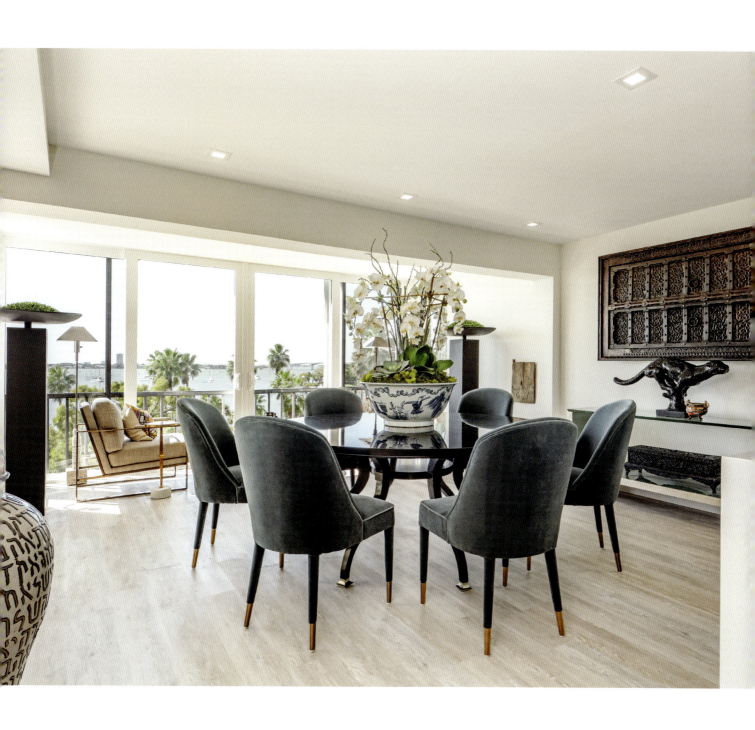

In this high-rise dining room with spectacular views of the water, I chose to forgo a chandelier altogether. The lacquered round table even reflects the view, and the tall zinc pedestals frame the windows and the dining area of the apartment. The rich teal velvet fully upholstering the dining chairs reflects the color of water at times of the day.

Eating is an action.
Dining is an experience.
Living well demands effort,
but the reward is a life well lived.

This Napa Valley dining room, for me, has quintessential California traditional styling. Rich details, custom woodwork, updated furniture pieces, banquette seating, and an oversized lantern in place of a chandelier all contribute to the aesthetic. It is sophisticated with a sense of formality, yet it exudes warmth, comfort, and history.

Dining is an essential element in the living-well equation. Living well is not about eating in the fanciest restaurants or how often you go out to dine; it's about how the experience enriches and satisfies all your senses. Restaurant design takes many cues from the home and vice versa. Open plans, where the kitchen and dining areas are visible, are now standard in both. Preparing food has become both a spectator sport and a group activity. The way we eat, what we eat, and how we eat have changed drastically. Today's open kitchen and dining areas are what I affectionately call the "bistro kitchen." This describes today's new kitchen designs, where the experience of cooking, serving, eating, and family life is all one. It can be as beautiful and dramatic as your imagination can conjure.

This dining room shares its space with the front door, the garden door, the staircase, and walkways through the kitchen and living room. It was imperative that the design leave room for flow and allow for the dining table to expand to seat a larger number of guests. Check!

If you grew up in a household like mine, great importance was placed on table manners. The combination of sit-down dinners and proper table manners was not always a fun one for me as a kid. I remember more than one battle that may or may not have led to me being sent from the table to my room. For better or worse, we now live in a more casual time, and our restaurants and dining habits have followed the trend.

Here are a few thoughts on dining and design in today's modern dining rooms:

Set the table and sit down. Sitting down with a plate, utensils, and a napkin can change your life.

Plate your food. This little trick is one I live by even when eating takeout. Taking the food out of the microwave container or out of the wrapper and placing it on a plate immediately elevates the experience . . . and the taste!

Have an array of options. One of the things I do just for myself is to keep a variety of dishware and tableware in my pantry so that no matter my mood or type of food, the meal is enlivened by the presentation. My Aunt Pat used to say, "A true gentleman uses a butter knife, even when dining alone." Try it; you'd be surprised how good it makes you feel.

Be eclectic. There was a time when buying dishes was a big deal. You went to a store, and you bought full place settings of your favorite china and crystal patterns. Today, we buy what we love and mix it up!

Make your choices personal. The best advice I can offer is to consider your table, chairs, server, and any other pieces as individuals. I love to mix the style and finish of a table with chairs of a different style. Nothing is more dramatic to me than a traditional table and modern chairs. The contrast makes both stand out.

Reimagine traditional furniture. The traditional breakfront displaying your fine china has become a thing of the past—but that does not mean you should just discard this beautiful piece of furniture. I love to reimagine a breakfront as a bookcase or bar cabinet in the living room.

Consider a new take on a server. One of my favorite pieces of furniture to use as a server is the Chinese altar table. They are usually quite long and as tall as a bar top, which makes them perfect for serving. Plus, they aren't as deep as a typical server, so they fit in dining rooms that may lack space for a table, chairs, and guests.

This dining room in a house on the National Register of Historic Places still needed to function as modern space. The furniture is a mix of styles, periods, and cultures. We retained all the original floors, the door, the fireplace, and details. The prayer screen mounted on the wall is used as a base to layer a second piece of original art. Both pieces are prized possessions from the owners' travels throughout Asia. The scale of the lantern speaks to both the tailored nature of the house and a sense of modernity in a home for today.

Left: To create this fabulous dining area in the open "bistro style" kitchen, I upholstered the chairs in black leather on the seat and black linen on the backs. The demilune server has an oversized fluted face. The buffet lamps are silver-leaf bamboo on crystal bases, and the art—both vintage and contemporary—is from the owner's private collection.

Right: New construction can make it difficult to create a sense of detailed style. Here I chose to add detail by selecting contrasting custom-made wallpapers with metallic accents. One paper is for the walls; the other is installed in the ceiling coffers. French-inspired sconces and art deco–style upholstered side chairs add richness and a sense of history to a new house.

Opposite: This modern California dining room is full of warm details, from the leather on the guest chairs and the traditional rug to the antique hay fork used as a table runner.

This light-filled breakfast room combines a custom modern quartz top table on a steel base with painted versions of both French- and English-style benches and chairs. The result is a totally new way of dining that is neither traditional nor contemporary.

This solarium was the perfect spot to add a more informal dining area in a very formal home. The natural light and spectacular view of the ocean make daytime dining an event. In this room, I chose to hang the large crystal chandelier from the center of the glass ceiling to illuminate the room and bring the attention to the highest peak of the room.

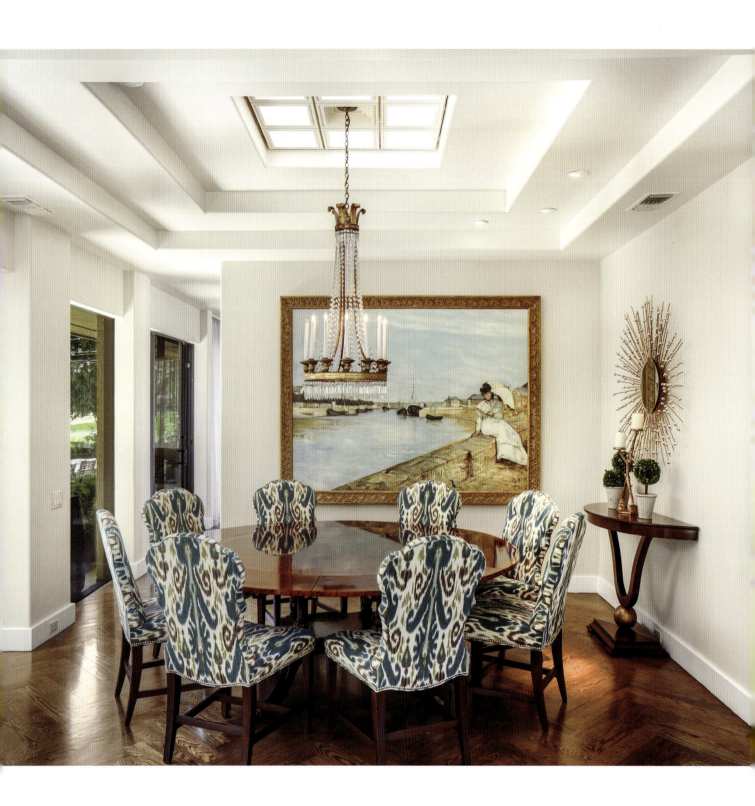

This dining room is a transitional space between the living room and club room. Even though this area is used as a passageway, I created a true sense of luxury and place with the selection of mixed periods, styles, and finishes for the room. The crowning glory is the fully restored seventeenth-century chandelier with its original water-gilt finish.

I am never afraid of what I call "substantial style." These two chandeliers in the same visual line don't fight each other; each makes the other more conscious of their importance.

I selected the server for its details and finishes as much as for the height. The higher surface makes serving easier. The antiqued mirror in the door panels keeps the large piece from overwhelming the small room. Don't worry about overlapping or intersecting the window. The light through this window and the sheer linen draperies frames the contrasting server perfectly.

There was no need for a large formal dining room for this second home. I defined the space with both the rich wall color and pieces of furniture with lots of visual and textural details. By contrasting the backs of the dining chairs with the patterned fabric and nail heads, it accentuates the shape of the chair and keeps it from blending in with the neutral table. The two extra-large reproduction French trumeau mirrors expand the small space and add sensational detail to the open room. They also reflect the original art on the inside wall of the room to the rest of the great room.

CHOOSING A CHANDELIER

I cannot think of a single room where a chandelier would not heighten the style. All chandeliers have a voice. Is yours only whispering?

This art deco–inspired chandelier is detailed with glass bubbles. It is the perfect choice for the lower ceiling of this sitting room.

We all know about using chandeliers in the dining room, foyer, or even over the kitchen island. I love using them in any room and in any style, be it traditional or contemporary. I like to use them in as many spaces as possible, because they make a room feel extra special. Consider a chandelier for your powder room, mudroom, closet, or bathroom.

Hanging light fixtures fall into one of three categories: chandeliers, pendants, and ceiling-mount fixtures. In each case, being bold and dramatic is key to the success of the installation. My three parameters in choosing the proper fixture are placement, style, and scale.

The first consideration is always the placement and installation. No matter the room, does the chandelier hang openly and you pass under it, or does it hang over a piece of furniture? If you need to walk under the fixture, then obviously the height of the chandelier is the most important of your decisions. A large-scale ceiling-mount fixture can be both dramatic and livable because it sits closer to the ceiling, eliminating anyone banging their heads.

When hanging a chandelier over a table, first consider the shape of the table. When I am hanging over a round table, I like the diameter to be similar to that of the table. Usually within a few inches of the outside edge of the tabletop is enough. If I am hanging over a rectangular surface, I am careful not to let the arms of the chandelier overhang the edges of the table below.

This gorgeous old staircase has an equally beautiful crystal chandelier that I gave considerable warmth with the addition of the pleated tuxedo shades.

Above, left: Even a ceiling-mount fixture can be imposing. This flush-mount chandelier is more than 48 inches in diameter and forces you to take notice, even though it is not suspended from the ceiling above.

Above, right: An oversized lantern as a chandelier for a table or island is a statement that is both traditional and modern.

The style and scale of the chandelier are a matter of taste, but I always consider the visual weight and bulk of the chandelier as well. Sometimes I require something lighter in appearance with lots of air space between the frame and possible details. Other times, I'm looking for visual weight to command the viewer's attention. I often add miniature lampshades both to traditional and modern fixtures to diffuse the light and create an overall effect of warmth and romance. Have fun when selecting a chandelier, and never underestimate the power of whimsy when choosing.

This new chandelier takes its style cues from French antique fixtures. Instead of traditional cut crystal, these hanging decorative drops are flat plaques of mirror and give the fixture a sense of modernity.

Consider scale. The common issue I see in homes is that the chandelier is too small for the space. Many people become timid and believe that smaller is a safer choice. This happens to be one of those times when bigger is usually always better. We all know how disconcerting a sofa or sectional can be in a room when it is too large. The space feels dwarfed and cramped, and you can end up feeling that you have wasted your money and ruined the effect you were hoping to achieve in your home. With chandeliers it is best to take the approach that the light fixture is meant to be dramatic and therefore you should make a statement—and part of that statement is scale. I often choose a style of chandelier to contrast the overall feel of the room. In other words, I love using a modern fixture in traditional rooms and traditional fixtures in modern spaces. The juxtaposition of styles can enliven the décor of either.

The chandelier, pendant, or ceiling mount is a way of expressing your style and can be as unique as your personality. Don't settle on the first store or website you visit. Think out of the box and decide to go deeper than the "popular fixture" of the day. I love to hunt through both vintage and antique shops, as well as auction websites. Whether big or small I am searching for the unique, different, and dramatic. Add a coat of paint, some new mini-shades, or new ornaments or globes and you have a piece that is one of a kind to display with pride for years to come.

Above: I found this seventeenth-century French chandelier packed away in a warehouse, where it had been for decades. It still has its original water-gilt finish, so we made the decision to go through a painstaking restoration process of more than eight months. The result is a museum-quality piece to live with for generations, once again.

Left: This 60-inch LED chandelier demands attention and has forty-eight bulbs to create dramatic light effects.

Opposite: These aged glass lanterns were handmade in Venice. I gathered together the entire group and hung them in a scattered pattern at varying heights from a burnished gold tea paper ceiling.

Chapter 4

THE BEDROOM

For this guest suite in a warm-weather location, we added color and pattern to create a sense of luxury and style that would not feel suffocating. My trick for layering patterns is to be sure to vary the sizes of each. Mix and match, enjoy the freedom to create, and have some fun!

This bedroom sparkles like the finest hotel suite. Handmade wallpaper, a custom-made bed, monogrammed linens, and bed chests in a platinum finish are just some elements of this luxurious retreat.

A bedroom is meant to be an oasis from daily life. I create more than a place to simply sleep. I want the experience of your bedroom to be relaxing, luxurious, and restorative.

A personal indulgence of mine that I love to
share with clients is the use both of table
lamps and reading lamps over the bed.

Layering the hand-painted wallpaper with rich woven drapery fabric heightens the richness of this bedroom. And the cozy seating area only heightens the luxuriousness of the private suite.

During my career as a designer, I have never met a client who didn't tell me that they wanted a bedroom and bathroom as beautiful as the most elegant hotel suite they have ever occupied. Everyone wants their bedroom to be luxurious, calming, and restful.

Fortunately, there are specific guidelines that you can follow in creating the perfect bedroom. Here is how I create the private space that dreams are made of:

All beds need a headboard! College students are the few who can get away with making this bedroom faux pas. You can choose tall or short, upholstered, wood, metal, or a combination, but a headboard is a crucial (if not mandatory) element to a finished bedroom.

Use down mattress toppers. Getting into bed should be like lying on a cloud.

Create a retreat. Neutral is the easy choice, but a sense of calm can be created with color and pattern as well. Choose what you love.

Scent is everything. I use both linen spray on my sheets and scented candles in my room.

Comfortable seating is a must. It can be as simple as a bench at the foot of the bed or take the form of a seating area in your room.

A comforter always goes inside a duvet. Think of it as going out wearing only your socks. Better duvets have ties on the inside to hold your comforter in place, or you can add them yourself to make life easier.

All your lighting goes on dimmers. This includes bedside table lamps. Find plug-in dimmers for table lamps at your local hardware store or online.

Use window treatments everywhere. Window treatments are as important in the bedroom as anywhere else in a beautiful home. The difference is that I use blackout lining to ensure darkness.

Above: I like to make my clients feel like they are guests staying in a luxury hotel. In this room, beautiful bedding and mono-grammed sheets reflect off the silver mercury glass lamps to add shine and drama. I created a small entry moment by framing the window just inside the bedroom entrance with dramatic drapery, a pedestal, and an urn. I call it the guest suite foyer.

Ceiling fans are a standard in every climate, but they can have style too. This walnut version demands attention and coordinates with the wood of the bed. Always remember to go big with the size of your fan if you actually want to move air and to cool the room.

Opposite: For a high-rise primary bedroom on the water in sunny Florida, I gave both the bedroom and the ladies dressing room a view of the ocean. For added glamour, the front of the dressing table is filled with Swarovski crystals.

In this historic Charleston primary suite, I created a bedroom mixed with both masculine and feminine details to give both husband and wife a sense of ownership.

A paisley upholstered bed is fitted with a bespoke pinstripe duvet. Add a bit of navy velvet layered over blue-and-white gingham, and you have a bed to be shared. The center pillow is embroidered with the longitude and latitude of the exact location of the home. The floors, doors, details, and fireplace all are original to the house.

A bedroom suite should be a refuge. Soft, warm, and modern, this bedroom radiates a quiet luxury by blending neutrals in subtle patterns and window treatments created from bands of linen combined with silk scrim (a lightweight woven fabric similar to sheer) on electric drapery rods controlled from the bed or sitting area.

The fireplace has a custom stone surround.

The centerpiece of every bedroom is the bed. When clients ask me to give them a bed like the one at their favorite resort, what they are really asking for is a bed that looks and feels lush, inviting, and—of course—incredibly comfortable.

Once the mattress and the bed are in place, the real work of creating comfort and richness begins—time to select your bedding! It is essential to know the traditional components of a luxurious bed, and then you can pick and choose which elements best suit your dream.

The bed area of the same room is grounded by the custom-made metallic damask paper and upholstered bed. Luxury bedding is a staple in any bedroom I create. Falling into bed should feel like being swallowed by a cloud.

Knowing the elements of bedding will help you to define your own style. Let's get started . . .

Mattress: The perfect bed begins with the right mattress. I make sure that the fill, cover, and stitching all are organic material. I will not buy a mattress with any trace of formaldehyde (a common element in the fill), and neither should you.

Sheets (top sheet, fitted sheet, and pillowcases): Buy the very best quality that you can afford. Buy only all-natural thread sheeting. Forget about the thread count; it's the quality of the thread that matters.

Blanket (found above the sheets and under the coverlet): Choose content and weight for each season. Try wool for fall/winter and cotton for spring/summer. Silk or cashmere blankets are expensive, but they are lightweight and lavish and they moderate body temperature through each season.

Coverlet (found above the top sheet and blanket): This decorative item often takes the place of a blanket.

Duvet (an item used to cover your down comforter): The duvet is the actual cover, not the filler inside. A duvet is a traditional European bed item used to cover the comforter and take the place of the top sheet. Today, we often use both a duvet and a top sheet.

Comforter (an alternative to the duvet): Think of a comforter as a permanent duvet, because the fill does not come out. The fill is usually quilted between the top and bottom fabrics.

Bedspread (a cover for the entire bed that reaches the floor on three sides and encases the bed pillows at the top of the bed): This was the most common bedcover before the days of comforters and duvets.

Shams (pillow covers): Shams can be standard pillow sizes or Euro (26 by 26 inches). Shams often match your comforter or duvet, though I usually choose a secondary pattern for more interest and personality.

Decorative pillows (coordinated pillows for the bed): These pillows can be square, rectangular, boudoir, lumbar, or bolster. Use these favorites to your heart's content.

I approach guest bedrooms with the same vigor and eye for detail as any bedroom in a home. The success of a guest room hinges on covering all your bases. Beyond a beautiful and comfortable bed, I always include seating, a big mirror, and nightstands full of paper, pencils, magazines, and snacks. Plenty of good lighting for reading is imperative—and don't forget USB outlets, chargers for electronics, or both. I also love using electric shades and drapes controlled from the bed. Include plenty of hangers and towels, along with an iron and ironing board. Consider all the amenities of a fine hotel room and you are on the right track.

Chapter 5

ACCESSORIES

In the tableau for a cocktail table, I combined a modern piece of original porcelain with an antique English ink well. The silver-leaf pattern on the reverse side of the glass creates a modern platform for both items.

Trays are a favorite accessory of mine. I use them like a platform or pedestal to display on every surface. Try them as a way to gather like or contrasting items in the living room, kitchen, bathroom, and bedroom.

*Accessorizing is a form of storytelling.
You do not have to yell to get your point across.
It is not about how much you gather—it's
about the meaning behind it all.*

A timeless observation made by the great fashion designer Coco Chanel illustrates the importance of accessorizing—in fashion, home, and life. She is said to have observed that once a woman is fully dressed, including accessories, she should edit out one item before leaving home. How very wise!

Accessories, specifically for the home, are a challenge for many. Coming from a "more is more" aesthetic, I struggle with editing as much as anyone. Proceed with caution, but never with fear.

I have seen too many homes where the accessories are overdone. That is because they are everywhere. There are too many, in quantities so great they are hard to pass up or ignore. At the opposite end of the spectrum, too few accessories can underwhelm to the point of distraction. Factoring in issues of color, scale, and proportion, and it is easy to throw your hands up and surrender.

Use scale, color, and material—soft and hard, high and low. Consider it all, even the rug. The floor is an accessory too.

Eglomise is the art of reverse painting on glass. This cabinet is the perfect example of an accessory that is more than an item on a table.

Let me offer some guidance to keep you on the right path:

Start with your own treasures. Gather up all those things that have meaning. Then go through your closets and cabinets for those treasures that might have been lost or forgotten.

Layering is both a technique and an approach. Your tabletops and surfaces become more vibrant when layered with beautiful objects and mementos. Every surface becomes a stage to tell a story.

I love to say, "It's all in the mix." Combine the fine with the casual, the high with the low, and the soft with hard.

Collecting and displaying are two different endeavors with the same goal. The best way to display and bring importance to a collection of items is to gather them together in one area. The visual impact makes a greater statement and creates conversation.

Allow the eye to move left to right and up and down. Intersect and create space between objects to allow the eye to stop and admire.

Diversify your art. Art can be even more exciting when you mix both traditional and modern pieces, as well as traditional and modern framing styles. It is the mix and the contrast that enlivens each in your home.

Create a family-photo wall. I have rarely done a home without one! They work almost anywhere and create an instant sense of home and tradition. The exception is the dining room and the powder room—sometimes it's just as important to know when to say no.

This page: In this sunroom, I took my design cues from the clients' love of Africa. By bringing together treasured items from their past safaris and adding some equally exotic pieces from other cultures with custom-made sconces and a one-of-a-kind, hand-beaded wood chandelier, this private space becomes one with the marsh outside—and is a reminder of their time on the Serengeti.

Opposite: Accessories are not just about filling the room. The details of this dining room are also accessories. Repeating elements and imagery is accessorizing.

Accessories need to be carefully considered. Here are some factors to keep in mind:

The Investment. When it comes to your accessories and art, price is not the indicator of value. Buy what you love and what you can afford. Some of my favorite pieces to display are kids' drawings in elaborate frames.

The Love. Love what you buy; love what you choose to live with. Art and accessories are like the jewelry of a well-dressed room.

The Framing. It can make the most humble of choices into a masterpiece. Presentation is everything!

The Mix. When creating your collection or displaying one, mix a variety of mediums. Combine framed pen-and-ink drawings, sketches, oils, acrylics, photography, and sculpture. One of my other guiding principles for accessorizing is to consider every detail of your room an accessory. It is more than the stuff and doodads on your coffee table; it includes every detail that makes the room. Consider how the nail-head trim on a chair or sofa accentuates the shape of the piece and how that sets off the fabric. The same can be said for details throughout the room. The relationships created between the pieces, the accessories, and the details are what create a memorable and meaningful home.

Opposite: I used this bookcase (one of a pair) in a dining room. The lower drawer portion holds trays, serving pieces, and linens. In the upper shelves is a mix of family and favorite pieces, along with leatherbound classics, all from the client's own collection, to define and brighten the shelves.

This custom marble pedestal is as much an accessory to this tableau as the vase or the original photography from Venice. The linen sheer frames both the windows and the vignette.

Accessories are every element of your room. Layers, patterns, textures, and details—they all tell the story. Natural elements, such as the goat skin of this upholstered waterfall cocktail table, are unique showstoppers.

Pillows are one of the most common room accessories. When selecting your own, be very conscious of materials. In this room, I used cashmere knit to create pillows of absolute luxury. They don't need to have a fabric pattern to make them memorable.

Dramatic statements can be made with accessories. Scale and color make all the difference. This antique jade foo dog is as dramatic (and as heavy) as they come.

Opposite: In this contemporary living room, the accessories are purposefully traditional and antique. The client wanted a modern living space full of warmth and interest. Even the art, though distinctly modern, is imagery of ancient coins.

Top: This dressing room already has a fabulous view of the water, so I used a custom Lucite pedestal to display a trio of hand-beaded hats from South America. The effect is that the hats almost appear to float, and the view is undisturbed.

Bottom: I took this antique monastic candlestick and transformed it into an electrified floor lamp. By using a chocolate-brown paper shade and an oversized silk tassel as an accessory, I increased both the fresh style and "glam" quotients of the piece.

In a room with little wall space for large art, an easel is a perfect display piece. In this living room, the contemporary easel allows the portrait to appear to be floating within the space. I paired the antique carved chair from the portrait with the original chair in the modern room.

In this foyer, I began by adding a floor-size blue-and-white porcelain vase to the presentation table. I created a colossal floral arrangement that was tall enough to go through the chandelier overhead. The overall effect is almost 10 feet tall!

For a designer showhouse in Texas, I created a gentleman's retreat filled with art, both traditional and modern, and paired the collection with an antique rug, a zebra hide, and an art deco–style mirrored screen. The "Broken Eggs" wall sculptures are from my Dann Foley Lifestyle collection for the Phillips Collection.

Midcentury architecture meets fresh midcentury-inspired style. Antiques can be the perfect complement to modern design.

Opposite: Details that make a room come from every direction. Consider every surface an opportunity to make a statement. The vignette we created here utilizes all the design tools of the trade: layering, color, texture, material, scale, style, period, and lighting. Together, these elements create a memorable moment in an even more memorable room.

Above: One of my favorite ways to accessorize a bathroom is with furniture. It is so unexpected. The scale of these lamps and mirror creates a true sense of grandeur in this bath.

Chapter 6

THE BATHROOM

Adding real furniture and original art pieces to your bathroom creates a strong sense of luxury. Everything is now more than just decorative; it becomes a deeply personal space of indulgence.

*What is more personal or intimate
than the bathroom of a home?
For me, beautiful bathrooms are as
much about a feeling as they are about
the materials and products.*

I used frosted glass doors for the commode
and the walk-in shower in the lady's
bathroom. A skylight placed in each space
allows the doors to glow throughout the day.
The built-in mirror is framed in the same slab
Italian porcelain that is used as baseboard
and doorframes throughout the bathroom.

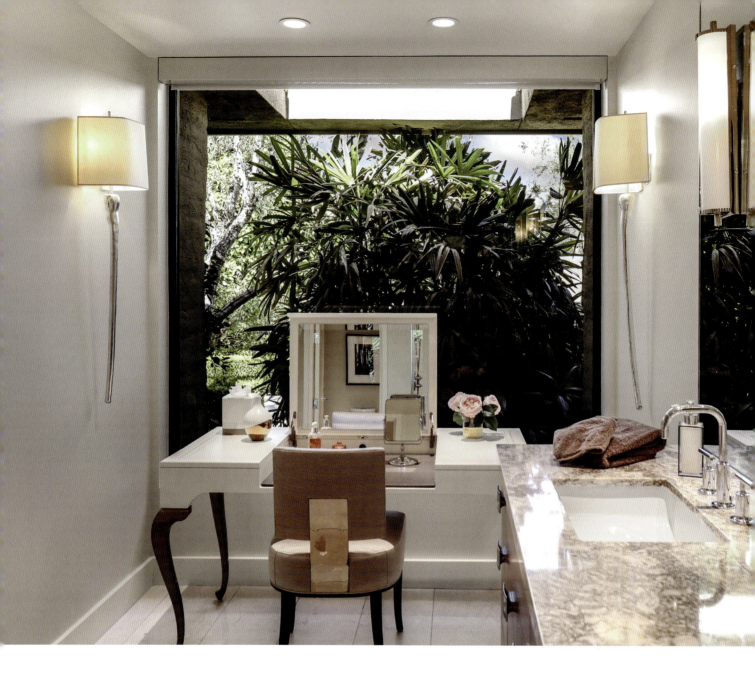

As a natural extension of your bedroom, the bathroom should be approached with the same care and eye for luxury and comfort. Like every space in your home, your bedroom and bath should tell a story of you. This is the most essential element to creating a bathroom, or a home, and it can indeed be the most intimate and inspired.

I like to make sure that a guest suite bathroom has all the amenities: plenty of luxurious towels within arm's reach, a makeup table, and plenty of light—both natural and man-made.

Here are some of my favorite strategies for designing a bath:

Whenever possible, add actual pieces of furniture to your bathroom. A small chair, stool, or side table by your tub is easy to incorporate, and it adds an extra sense of opulence and detail.

Add fresh flowers. A simple bud vase on the counter can really brighten your day!

Select a beautiful tray for your countertop to help contain the clutter. Creating order can be attractive.

Choose your towels wisely. I use only white/neutral towels of the best cottons because they are so soft and absorbent. The white means you can bleach them and keep them crisp and clean.

Install a shower wand and hose. This is one of the easiest ways to update an older shower. You can actually do it yourself, and not only does it add a "spa" element to your tub/shower, it makes the shower easier to clean.

Opposite: The ultimate luxury just might be the lady's bath in a primary suite with his-and-her baths! For the lady of house, it was all femininity with the handmade wallpaper, slipper tub, and vanity with a beauty station. Custom cabinets and furnishings add depth to the detailing. The custom round settee floats under a modern version of a French-style chandelier.

The walk-in shower is skylit from above to light the marble and mirrored tile mosaic we created by hand, along with a marble bench.

This primary suite bathroom for a high-rise apartment was designed with a European-style wet room. The custom vanity area is separated by a wall of frameless glass, which leads to a fully tiled room where both the shower and the standing tub are located. With plenty of room to move around, it creates a larger, more open space for bathing.

I commandeered space under a staircase to create a powder bathroom for this client. By tiling all the walls, I made room for an open shower under the stairs. I created a vanity from an antique Chinese pedestal and glass vessel sink. The client made the stained-glass mirror over the sink. The gilded iron sconce with flower vase stands directly opposite the door, so that when left open, there is an interesting and beautiful art display to view from the foyer.

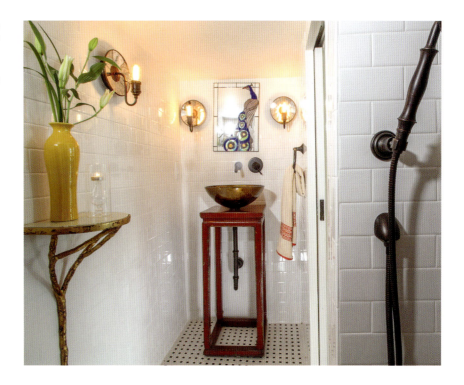

When it comes to materials for a bathroom, I like the modern approach to traditional selections. Stone slabs are really great, but today we have options that don't stain. Slab porcelain or quartz has all the beauty of stone without the maintenance issues. I like using it on shower walls too. It gives me the opportunity to eliminate grout lines and add the luxury of slab to the vertical bathroom surfaces.

Keeping hardware interesting is at the heart of a beautiful bathroom, but it also needs to be easy to care for. Finishes matter. Polished finishes are more difficult to maintain because they need to be wiped. Matte finishes are easier because they don't always show water spots as easily.

Dark-colored finishes on faucets, sinks, and fixtures are an issue with hard water. They spot easily and can stain permanently over time. There is a reason why the black sinks and commodes of the 1980s have fallen out of favor. The same can be said for brass and copper; water spots are a given on that high-polish finish. Those metal finishes can also be hammered or aged to make them more manageable. My advice is to use these materials for sinks in places where they are more for display and get less use.

Using furniture is one of my favorite bathroom details. By using both new and antique furniture in this case, I upped the style and luxury quotients exponentially. The custom paneling in the niche articulates the richness of such an intimate space. The oversized steam shower was created with slabs of sparkling quartz, and the glass enclosure with its frosted modesty screen provides the user a sense of privacy without closing in the space.

This guest suite bathroom is outfitted with both color and pattern. By using multiple shades of blue in the design, the color now becomes the neutral in this space. A custom navy-blue vanity sits opposite the walk-in shower, with a feature wall of patterned concrete tile.

For a historic home, I designed a bathroom that was appropriate to the architecture and age of the house but fitted with modern luxuries. A new custom double vanity is placed against the window wall, where we created custom suspended mirrors, which allow the natural light to shine through. The vanity area acts as a central space with her dressing room on one side and the bathroom with shower, standing tub, and commode found on the opposite side. White marbles, porcelain wall tiles, an antique linen cabinet, and snow leopard carpeting all come together to create a truly unique and luxurious bath.

This page: This charming old home still needed a luxurious primary bathroom. We began with natural-wood-finished porcelain tile floors. The extra-wide vanity is custom made and custom colored. I added light and retained privacy by installing clerestory windows both in the bathroom and the wet room. In keeping with the age and style of the Spanish farmhouse, I designed shower walls to mimic traditional paneling. A series of handmade tiles in different shapes and details were laid out to create baseboard, crown, picture frame, and wainscot molding. The various shapes and details are unified through the same finish. The aged brass finish of the his-and-her bath fixtures adds to the vintage vibe.

Opposite: This is an example of how even the smallest of bathrooms can be dramatic. For this primary bathroom, we had to ensure a sense of luxury so that the small space did not disappoint. The vanity wall is tiled from floor to ceiling in a marble-and-brass mosaic. The vanity itself floats and is lit from underneath. The framed mirror lights with a touch of the finger, and the integrated sink and counter help expand the visual and physical limitations of the bathroom.

THE POWDER ROOM

A Jewel Box of a Bathroom

I like to put equal effort into the design of powder rooms as I do into the home's other bathrooms. As the one space in your home that literally all your guests will see, it had better be memorable. The powder room is an opportunity for clients to experiment and make bold statements. I approach the space as a laboratory for design and color.

Opposite: This powder room is a modern sanctuary, with a custom suspended vanity that acts as a floating bridge with a vertical wall panel in the same wood. The backlighting accentuates the architectural nature of the installation. Bold wallpaper, beautiful lighting, gold and bronze fixtures, and a lighted mirror are elements both of sophistication and style.

Left: This powder room is in the same client's primary residence. That home is traditional and formal. For the lady's powder room, we created an anteroom for a moment of respite. Combined with the mirrored art deco–style dressing table, the hand-carved chair, soft upholstery, substantial woodwork, original leaded-glass window, and opulent wallpaper and window treatment have perfectly set the tone of a luxurious inner sanctum.

Chapter 7

THE KITCHEN

A kitchen with a view! I decided to forgo the standard upper cabinet in favor of light, the view, and a sense of openness. Any storage lost was reclaimed through the new walk-in pantry just beyond the island.

The entire design for this kitchen began with a custom periwinkle-colored French La Cornue range.

If the kitchen is truly the "heart of the home," then shouldn't the choices in creating your kitchen be in the forefront of your thoughts in design, detailing, and budget? A kitchen is serious business!

itchens are a significant investment of money, sweat, and tears. They are the type of design that should be lasting. By most industry standards, a kitchen design should last fifteen years or more. In real life, it is not uncommon for a kitchen design to last more than twenty-five years (allowing for the occasional appliance replacement). A kitchen is the most expensive space in your home, as well. The costs of cabinetry, counters, and appliances are through the roof, so making the right decisions is crucial.

For this historic house kitchen, I wanted the kitchen's style and pieces to blend seamlessly with the rest of the house. I first opened the wall between the kitchen and the dining room for a more modern way of living.

Three decades of ever-changing kitchen design has taught me many things. Here are some of them:

The all-white kitchen is now the tired choice. Today's kitchens offer color, finishes, and wood stains like never before. Think outside the box and mix your cabinet selections. Do a different style and finish of cabinetry for your island or do one cabinet style and finish for the base cabinets and another for the upper cabinets. Mix traditional cabinet styles with more clean-lined contemporary versions for an updated transitional feel.

Stainless steel is the go-to appliance finish of choice, but today we have a wide range of colors to choose from. The trick is to keep color choices sophisticated and grown up and out of the "kitsch" zone. Use color as a base; it will become your neutral.

Coffee stations and wine bars are now standard equipment. They are the new must-have appliances. With the kitchen usually open to the great room, the preparation, plating, and serving of food is part of the party. A wine chiller with glass-front cabinets located above for stemware is a beautiful option. Drinking coffee is practically a national pastime, so creating a bespoke location for the preparation and serving of this all-day beverage is also a big plus for a new kitchen. Both built-in and freestanding coffee/espresso/cappuccino makers are the rage. Just make sure to have ample space for the storage of cups, mugs, and all the accoutrements that go with today's coffee obsession.

I always choose a microwave drawer rather than the wall installation. The microwave is one appliance I simply don't want to see in one of my gorgeous kitchens. It goes beneath the counter and slides out at the touch of a button. Choose a model with flip-down controls on the top edge so you don't have to crouch to see the settings and timer.

If you like to cook, I always recommend a single-bowl sink. The divided versions just don't have enough room for washing pots and larger pieces. And one side always gets that "gunk" in the drain that you have to get out with your hands. Yuck!

Under-cabinet lighting is critical to creating usable work surfaces and to the overall look of a finished kitchen. However, you should also consider lighting above the upper cabinets and at the toe kick base of your cabinets. They both are surprisingly beautiful details, and sensors can be added so toe kick lighting will come on automatically as a terrific night light for your kitchen.

I kept the design details traditional, with a twist for modern living.

Today's great-room kitchens have a responsibility to be beautiful. This contemporary kitchen also had to be glamorous enough for the open dining room. I chose sleek finishes on rich wood grains in two different colors of stain. Quartz counters and a marble and stainless-steel backsplash all add to the upscale design. The wine bar that separates the kitchen from the dining area makes for a handsome display cabinet, as well as containing wine coolers and a serving area. The crystal pendant over the island adds sparkle in addition to task lighting.

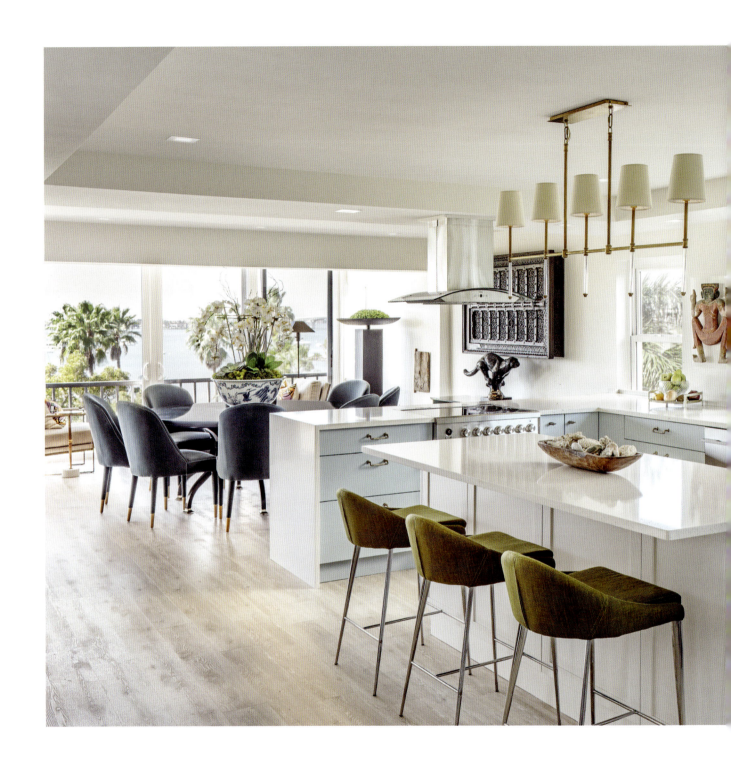

For this high-rise apartment, I chose to build the kitchen against a 14-foot window wall. The views in both directions are spectacular! Not only did the elimination of upper cabinets brighten and lighten the entire space, but I made up for the reduced storage by building a walk-in pantry at one end with a coffee station and its own window view from inside.

For this modern open-plan kitchen design,
we wanted to marry the design of each
portion of space to flow easily between
the work and entertaining areas. The
crowning glory was the gorgeous
figurative granite, which became an
eye-popping detail with its waterfall edge.
Even with all the beautiful interior details,
the room's view of the pool, golf course,
and mountains still holds center stage.

For this Northern California kitchen, we focused on the attached morning room. The décor and details of each space took cues from the other. We kept the palette soft but warm, the lines clean, and fussiness to a minimum. The details of the existing kitchen and furnishings created a cohesive and comfortable living/working kitchen.

Not every kitchen renovation has to begin with a complete demolition. This client wanted their winter retreat to be completed in a certain time frame. Once we realized that the cabinetry was all custom-built, we made the decision to salvage most of the design. I updated the appliances, counters, and backsplash. We made some adjustments to the cabinet layouts to provide more storage, and we added or changed all the lighting. By cutting back the sink peninsula and adding a waterfall side, we opened up the kitchen to the living space. The upper cabinets underwent a refinishing to visually raise the ceiling and bring a sense of lightness and transitional styling to the kitchen.

Chapter 8

TRAVEL & DESIGN

*Travel inspiration is more
than the souvenirs you buy.*

At Marie Antoinette's Petit Trianon there
remains the Hamlet, a working farm to this
day. Here, a bust sits atop a pedestal,
framed by a pair of French doors. The
texture and colors in the stone walls and
doorframes inspired a new color palette for
me to take home.

Inspiration is as much a moment and a feeling as it is physical.

No matter where I am traveling overseas, I make it a point to stop in Paris. The writer Gertrude Stein was said to have mused, "America is my country, but Paris is my hometown." I feel her presence in every step I take in this incredible city. Paris is my heart, and she speaks to me through my love of design and beauty.

Travel often goes hand in hand with collecting. My love of travel was instilled in me from an early age. The homes of my grandparents and parents were filled with items culled from trips to all corners of the globe.

One of my earliest memories is sitting at our breakfast room table on summer mornings as my mother read to us from my grandparents' travel itinerary. We knew from day to day where they were and what they would be doing or seeing. Summer was their travel season, and they would leave for two to three months at a time to tour the world.

Within weeks of their departure, we began to receive packages and crates of everything you can imagine: furniture, paintings, sculptures, textiles, and antiques. Even as a child, I was learning about the world and style through the treasures my grandparents collected. When they returned home, another treat awaited. My parents would take us to my grandparents' home, where my brothers, sister, and I would lie on the living-room floor, munching on fresh popcorn, as

A quiet street in Rome. Travel relaxes and
inspires me. The simplest of details can draw
me in. Color is my muse.

they shared the slides of their travels. We felt as if we were traveling the world right alongside them, as my grandfather spun his travel tales, one after another, immersing us in every detail of their experiences.

It was weeks after their return when changes began appearing in their home décor, as they added new pieces to their existing collections. I found it exciting to see how everything would fit in. I wanted to watch my grandparents and their decorator make the new items work. And work they did! They fit in flawlessly with the rest of the collections. My grandparents' home was a perfect reflection of who they were. Their home grew, changed, and evolved just as they did.

By bringing home pieces from your travels, near or far, you realize they are more than just mementos of your travels. They help you tell your story. You add another layer to your life through experiences you could not have had by staying home or by watching the travel shows on television.

Displaying a mix of pieces from different trips and cultures can be a difficult task. The trick is to bring like pieces together. Gathering similar items allows you to mix styles and origins for an arrangement that conjures fond memories and sparks conversation. I am giving you permission to experiment, to be playful, and to create a style for your home that speaks to the narrative of your life. Who are you? Where have you been? What has touched you and given meaning to your life?

Another place where I find great beauty and inspiration comes during my summer stop on Capri, Italy. Jackie Kennedy and the jet set of the 1960s made it famous, and it's the natural beauty and the incredible generosity of the people that brings me back year after year. The local craftspeople astound me on every visit.

The big picture can be breathtaking, and the details are the bits and pieces that inspire meaningful, personalized design.

Opposite, top: This image is a perfect tableau to summer on Capri: the gates of a private villa; a vintage car with woven rattan side panels; a big, beautiful terra-cotta pot; and a view of the sea beyond. This spot actually stopped me in my tracks on my early-morning run. Luckily, I had my phone to capture it!

Right: When I think of detailing the architecture of new homes today, I often conjure pictures of the Colosseum and its symmetry. The repetition of the openings, arches, and materials is still used every day. I am a lover of symmetry; it is a mainstay in my approach to all interiors and exteriors.

Opposite, bottom left: The ruins of the Roman Forum are haunting. I am struck by its artistry, yet I feel a great sense of loss wandering its streets. Modern Rome rises all around, and the Colosseum is at one end. Two worlds collide to create a new way of living. A whole new style is found in the mix.

Opposite, bottom right: The architecture of the Louvre in Paris is as beautiful and impressive as the art it houses. Before it was a museum, it was the royal residence, and Napoleon III's apartments are still intact. Art, architecture, and ornamentation—they are my basis for creating great interiors. The French have a certain knack for bringing together the past and the present in a way that allows each its own statement as one enhances the other. The glass-and-steel pyramid entrance to the Louvre is a perfect example. The same can be true for your home. Live with what you love. Do not allow yourself to be stuck in one place or one time or one style.

And, remember, travel is more than the physical things you brought home with you. The inspiration you find can last a lifetime. I have been known to fall in love with a doorknob or the shape of a chairback. The littlest of details can inspire and cause a lasting shift in the way we see our world. Once you experience the life-changing shift in perspective that travel can create, you will never be able to look at anything in the same way again.

In the South of France one summer, some friends and I took a beautiful house in Ax-les-Thermes, with a working vineyard surrounding the property. Every morning, I walked through the vines and wondered at the incredible colors in nature. This is where great design begins for me. The small village allowed me the opportunity to slow down, experience simple beauty, and allow it to inspire me for a full year of busy client meetings. It filled me with moments of incredible inspiration.

Above: One of the great things about traveling through ancient cities is finding, and then importing, fragments for my clients. They are abundant! I just let my mind's eye play with the possibilities.

Right: The open ceiling of the Parthenon is one of the great architectural wonders of the ancient world. To this day, I keep images of it in my office to serve as inspiration for windows, doorways, ceilings, and floor patterns.

The architecture and light of Italy are a constant source of inspiration for me in my work. For me, truly great design is based on tradition. In my most-modern designs, I find a basis in the past. The trick is knowing when to follow the guidelines offered and when to throw caution to the wind. This is where authentic personal design and style find their start.

This quiet French church near Cannes is a far cry from the film world and the movie star madness of the world-renowned film festival. It represents summertime in the South of France for me: blue sky, palm trees, symmetry, stone, and devotion. How can something so beautiful still be so pious? In my work, I try to fuse the grand with the humble. This fusion is what every home should be. It should fill your senses, speak to your passions, and embrace you lovingly. It is the lifestyle I seek when traveling abroad.

The Belvedere pavilion in the gardens of the Petit Trianon was created for Marie Antoinette on the grounds of Versailles. This is one of many follies built to enrich the senses and transport you as you wander the gardens. Quiet little corners or moments in design give a home a sense of intimacy. We all need those places to curl up and be still. Being soothed and embraced by your home is always the goal.

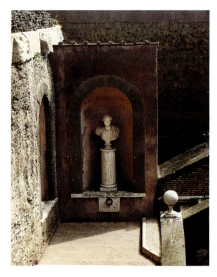

This is a secluded interior courtyard at the Castel Sant'Angelo in Rome. It was first a tomb; then for more than three hundred years, it was the residence for the pope (before the Vatican). I love to sit, surrounded and embraced by these ancient stairs made from ancient stone. I am always reminded that beautiful things are not ours; we do not own them. Rather, we possess them for a period, and then, if they are lucky, they live on to help tell someone else's story.

This lower hallway in Versailles offers a neutral palette among the opulence and excess that is the palace. It is a moment of visual respite. The simplicity speaks volumes to the engineering of the palace.

The inside of the dome of Napoleon's tomb in Paris. You have to wonder at the talented hands that created all of this. Then, apply that same thought in your own home. Live with what you love!

A garden house at the Palace of Versailles. I was mesmerized by the intricacy and layers of lattice work and the shades of green. It reminds me that monochromatic design does not have to mean only neutrals.

A long cobblestone driveway, framed in massive old shrubbery, becomes other-worldly in the rain. I have walked this drive many times over the years in France. The beauty of it in the rain is almost overwhelming. It made me dream of glazed tiles made by hand for a project waiting at home.

Bread is a staple of life in all cultures. Not only have the French made the making of bread an art form, but even a simple bread display on the street becomes a rich still life.

A staircase in a private residence in Paris. And this is considered the service stairs! *La beauté de la vie*—the beauty of life.

Chapter 9

BEFORE & AFTER

*Cinderella was the ultimate makeover
fantasy, and we are all still trying to
live up to the dream. Re-creating the
place you live also has the added value of
reinventing how you live. It is more than
a dress and pumpkin coach: it is a life
renewed, reinvented, and invigorated.*

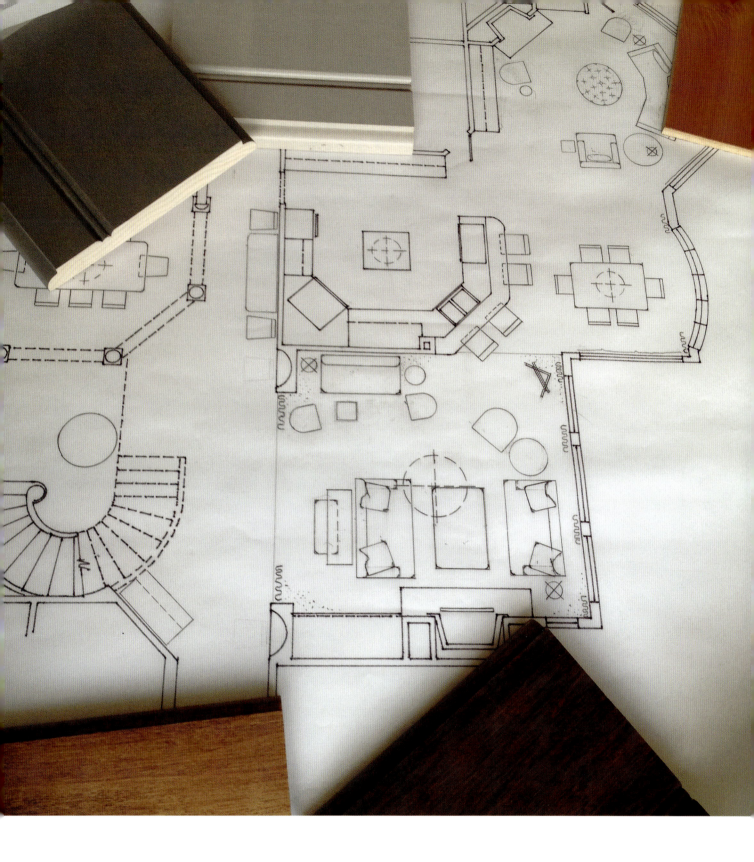

Every great design begins with a plan. Major renovations, like those shown here, have a great deal of background and effort in every detail before the job of transforming a home can begin. Drafting, sketching, and sourcing materials all create a clear picture. The plan is the key to the most successful home renovations.

elevision and the internet have made the Before & After experience some of the most sought-after imagery around. Magazines will tell you that the annual Before & After–themed issue is the most popular issue of the year, and I can tell you that the analytics on our firm's website is a testament to the enduring popularity of these images of transformation. We know that people who visit our website actually spend as much time poring over the Before & After section of the site more than every other section combined! There is something so exciting and infinitely inspiring about seeing a room's potential fully realized. How could I create a book about creating your best life through design, without showing you some truly remarkable transformations?

The trick to creating a truly magical makeover is to step back and to clear your mind of what you know and of all your preconceived notions of what the space is or has been. To completely reimagine a space takes courage. One way to start the process is to flip the point of view of your room. Point your furnishings and focus in a different direction. As I have said earlier in the book: perspective is everything. Redirecting attention is the easiest way to see your space in a new way. Sometimes the new direction may even result in changing the way you use a room. I turn dining rooms into libraries, storage rooms in theaters, closets into wine rooms, and spare rooms into glamorous dressing rooms. A makeover is what you make it. Your spaces should serve your needs and desires.

Wildly successful makeovers often use pieces and items that you might not have considered for the space in the past. An easy example is hanging a lantern in place of a chandelier in your dining room or kitchen. I have also repurposed desks as dressing tables, pretty trash cans as planters, table runners as elongated place mats spanning kitchen islands, rugs as tapestries, and mantelpieces as headboards. I can go on all day about creative uses for everyday items, but my point is this: a makeover is more than just new things. It is a way of thinking anew about existing space. You don't have to move to create the home you always wanted. Chances are you already have the space waiting to be reimagined.

BEFORE

Putting aside the fact that everything in this dining room was brown, all the furniture was also clunky and too big for the dining space. The answer was to vary both the scale and finish of each piece. The pair of reproduction French trompe l'oeil mirrors reflects the equally large-scale painted silk chandelier from Venice, Italy. The custom chairs circle the pedestal table in a pale floral fabric on the chairback that surrounds diners. The server is set at bar height with Regency-styled door panels set with mercury glass mirror.

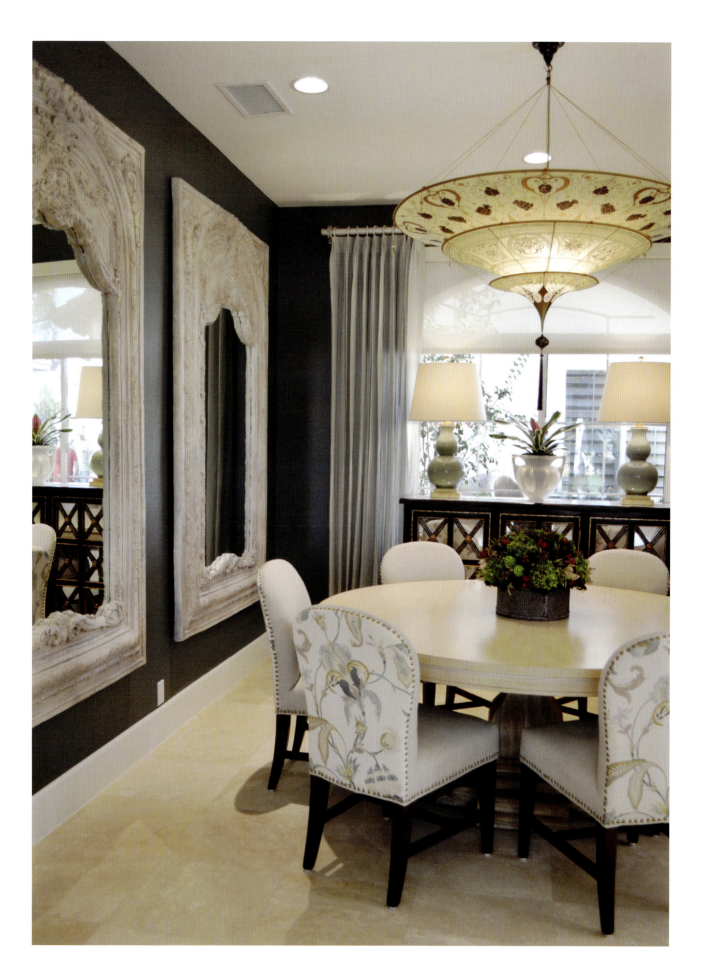

BEFORE

I am the fresh pair of eyes a homeowner often needs to reimagine an existing space. I find that most people don't need to move to achieve the lifestyle goals they are seeking. Perspective is everything. Beyond new furnishing and paint, one of the easiest ways to reinvent your living space is to change the focus. Try a new direction for your furnishings, and you gain a whole new point of view in an existing room.

BEFORE

With its dark and heavy stone wall, this dining room felt oppressive. The hard furnishings only added to the feeling of discomfort. We took all the stone out, and I designed paneling for the wall with a custom mural in the large panels. The large lantern accentuates the height of the room and creates a dramatic and transitional style for this traditional room. The custom-built banquette is a wonderful way of making a more formal dining room feel cozy. In lieu of cabinets, I chose bookcases to flank the dining table and display beloved family items and books. The drawers below are perfect for storing flatware, linens, and serving pieces.

Kitchens are a huge investment. When I can save good elements, I do. In this kitchen, I actually kept all the custom handmade wood cabinets. What really needed updating were the color, the use of soffits, and the counters and fixtures. I lightened the overall feel of the kitchen by refinishing the upper cabinets in a custom lighter finish, eliminated the soffits, replaced the counters, and added the waterfall countertop. The island lantern gives this transitional kitchen a dash of chic.

BEFORE

BEFORE

A kitchen can be an extremely daunting and expensive undertaking. No matter what you do, it is a big investment. In this kitchen I first decided to leave the services (water, drains, electric) in place to save time and money. I chose two different cabinet finishes—in this case Italian laminates—to contrast the upper cabinets from the lower and pantry-style cabinets. The new wine bar is the bridge between the kitchen prep area and the kitchen dining area. The glamorous island fixture allows this dramatic kitchen to play to the equally dramatic living and dining rooms in this great-room design.

Bedrooms are a particular favorite of mine. In this case, we took a dark and dreary room and created that perfect retreat everyone is always asking me to design. I removed the soffits surrounding the room and lightened the palette. The immediate effect made the room feel larger and the windows bigger, even though I did not do any major construction to the existing space. The molding details and handmade wallpaper ground the bed and create a dramatic backdrop to the furnishings and lighting.

BEFORE

The opposite side of this same master suite benefited from the soffit removal and palette change as well. An oddly placed and badly detailed fireplace was removed in favor of a cozy seating area with a custom banquette designed to hug the corner.

BEFORE

Bedrooms are vitally important to living well. They should be comfortable, warm, inviting, and beautiful/handsome. Any bed without a headboard is an affront to good taste and gracious living. If you want to renovate your bedroom, start with a bed that you will love to look at and climb into. I design bedrooms to be spaces that you don't want to leave. Isn't that what makes a bedroom successful?

I like to approach the design of a walk-in closet as more than a mere storage space. I put the same amount of consideration and detail into a closet as I do the rest of the bedroom. I create dressing rooms. This walk-in closet was quite large, but the storage design was dwarfed and wasted at least half the usable space. By taking advantage of the room's height, I more than doubled the amount of storage and organized it with custom-built cabinetry in a mix of finishes. The marble floor, wallpaper, crystal light fixtures, carpet, and custom ottoman (which is also a clothes hamper) are the kind of extra details that make the room not only more beautiful but also more fully functional for its purpose. I want you to be happy while you're dressing and getting ready for the day.

BEFORE

I face too many great rooms where well-intentioned contractors act as the designer. In this case, the combination of the dark tile, its scale, and the tiny fireplace box created an eyesore in this dated room. I removed all the cabinetry and slate tile, enlarged the firebox, and added an appropriately styled and scaled surround. The result is a fireplace that is gracious and handsome in a newly decorated room full of comfortable custom furnishings and original art.

BEFORE

BEFORE

The dreaded fireplace niche is a particular issue in many homes. My approach is to add more than just a console. In this home, we first addressed the back wall by making a custom paper mural based on the wall of a crumbling building. The custom cabinet and shelves all are floating and lit from the bottom to magnify the contemporary installation. By backlighting the area, it also accentuates the mural and makes both the niche and fireplace wall appear larger.

The view from the opposite end of this great room illustrates how the use of furniture arrangements and decorative and architectural details can transform the way a room looks and feels. It is more than just beautiful; it is functional beauty.

BEFORE

BEFORE

Opposite: This dark and dreary sitting room with its imposing and equally dark stone fireplace needed to be reinvented. By stripping the stone and designing an entirely new hearth, surround, and chimney, I lightened both the physical and psychological effects of this eyesore. The fireplace is not any smaller; it is simply less obtrusive in the room. A brighter palette and window treatments designed to frame the view and furnishings, both traditional and modern, make for a room my clients want to enjoy and share.

The other side of the same sitting room offers you a chance to see just how complete the renovation actually was. The room now exudes charm and graciousness. All the furnishings were created and arranged to invite you to sit and relax.

This page: This sad bathroom with its low ceiling was ready for a complete redo. We could not physically raise the ceiling, so I decided to make you forget about it through very careful material selections and lighting. The metallic glass of the shower's feature wall is now the focus.

BEFORE

BEFORE

This transitional-styled bathroom was full of dated builder details. From the heavy soffits and the dark cabinetry to the massive tub deck, it screamed the 1990s. The time had come to re-create the large space and make it a true sanctuary to luxury and self-indulgence. By removing the soffits, we created an even higher ceiling. Installing a free-floating tub in the center of the room, we created a sense of more space and indulgent gratification. The custom cabinetry, glass bubble chandelier, custom Italian wall murals, accessories, sconces, and little hidden details—such as the electric window shade and outlets inside the vanity drawers—all stayed true to my bathroom ideal of luxury and convenience.

BEFORE

BEFORE

Today's restaurants take their design cues from residential design. I have included this remodel of a Palm Springs restaurant to illustrate just how a layered, detailed approach to any space can create the story and history you seek in your own home. The dining room is designed to be memorable, but also to feel like an intimate private room. The burnout sheers lend privacy between the booths I designed. Pattern, color, original fine art, and lighting combine to create something completely new. The lanterns are each handmade and one of a kind from Venice, Italy. Meanwhile, renovations to the ladies' bathroom turned it into a truly Instagram-worthy space!

Chapter 10

THE BUDGET

*Fantasy and reality can coexist.
All it takes is the right plan to
articulate the melding of desires
with realism.*

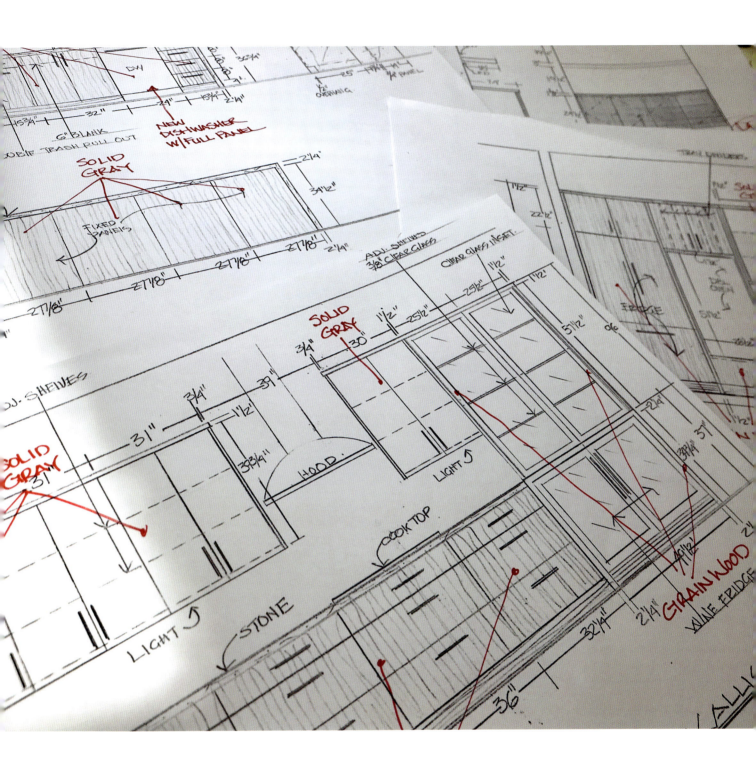

The plan and budgeting go hand in hand.

GROUNDING YOUR DREAMS IN THE REALITY OF YOUR BUDGET

by Beau Stinnette, principal
Foley & Stinnette Interior Design

For all of the beautiful design presented in this book, the big question remains: how much does it all cost? Here is something that we know for certain: it does not matter what amount you have set aside for your home; it never seems to be enough. For all the tips and tricks Dann has shared in these pages, it still comes down to budgeting for all of your needs, dreams, and desires.

Dann mentioned earlier in the book the importance of creating a plan before you begin. The scaled floor plans with your chosen furniture layouts and decorative selections are only half the equation, however. You might say that the design is the fantasy portion, and the budget the reality piece. The plan can be executed in as many steps as are

comfortable for you, but knowing what you want and what it will cost is crucial to your success. For our part, we take our clients' money very seriously. Avoiding costly missteps or mistakes should be one of the main reasons for hiring a professional design firm like ours.

When creating a budget for our clients, we take a two-pronged approach: the decorative and the contracting. They are built simultaneously. One does not exist without the other.

So where do you put your money? Where do you splurge and where do you go easy? We divide and conquer—and then bring it all together.

This is how we do it:

DECORATIVE BUDGET

List each room and each item in those rooms. Working with subtotals for each room is an effective way to keep financial perspective. You will spend more on rooms such as the living/family rooms and primary bedroom suites, and less on others, such as guest rooms.

Each room needs that one "Wow!" piece. A "Wow!" piece can be an incredible console for your living room or a one-of-a-kind screen for your foyer or a strong statement bed. Whatever it is, that "Wow!" piece will most likely be more costly than the other elements of the room. That piece is a focal point of the room. Then, we are more careful with expenditures on the rest of the elements, to balance out the total cost.

Be sure to list decorative items beyond furnishings. This includes items such as window treatments, including drapery hardware. We list wallpaper as a decorative item, but the installation is included in the contracting budget.

Allot for accessories. We generally will derive an accessory budget equal to 10 percent of the total decorative budget. That gives us a working number that we can divide as needed. This way we can splurge on a specialty item as long as we keep the total accessory budget in line. When it comes to accessories, I always go for unique, special items. It is better to have fewer, more important pieces than a bunch of "things." I can't overstate the importance of fine accessories.

Don't forget that shipping/handling/delivery and warehousing costs are separate yet are still part of the decorative budget. Our rule of thumb is to estimate 15 percent of your total decorative purchases to cover shipping and handling. Many manufacturers require delivery to a local warehouse where they have a loading dock and are able to unload their freight. This is a very important component of the budget, because it is also where inspection of each item takes place. It is better to find issues before your installation.

CONTRACTING BUDGET

List each room and then each task to be completed. Break the renovation down by room, just like you did with the decorative budget.

Don't forget demolition and debris removal. If demolition is involved (and it always is), that is its own line item, as is hauling away debris.

List each task separately. Demolition, electrical work, plumbing, carpentry, drywalling, painting and wallpapering, and other types of work should all be listed as separate items. By doing this, you won't leave anything out. Budget oversights can be deadly to a project!

There is no set percentage you can put on your budget items. Some rooms might require more electrical work, while others might need more plumbing or cabinetry. You have to approach each room individually.

It is quite common to be invoiced for "surcharges." These are often put on shipping or fuel costs or both (they can even apply to decorative items). Be sure to always have a total price for all the work in your budget.

Renovations can quickly become a can of worms. You don't know what is inside those floors, walls, and ceilings until you open them. We take the approach of hoping for the best and planning for the worst. Having said that, we recommend a separate budget line equal to 25 percent of the total as a "just in case" fund. You don't have to spend it, but if you need to, you will be glad it is there!

A Palm Springs condo designed for Southern California style, comfort, and fun!

The sum total of all your decorative purchases and contracting items is your budget. You may approach your budget from either direction. That means you can first come up with a number you do not want to exceed, or you can create a budget that fits your needs and desires and proceed from there. Either way, you want to achieve a comprehensive understanding of each space. Then you can make informed decisions as to how many phases you might need and how to finance all the changes.

The budgeting part of the process can be daunting and even downright depressing. Don't let it get you down! I can assure you that compromise is part of every project, on every level. We all make choices in life every day. There is no such thing as an unlimited budget. The process is part of the pleasure of creating your most magical home.

Keep in mind, the main objective is to finish the project, and the way to finish is to execute your plan by always moving forward. You don't have to complete your home overnight, but as long as you find yourself accomplishing tasks, both big and small, you will find the satisfaction in knowing you are creating a home that is as personal as it is stylish.

ACKNOWLEDGMENTS

There are so many people I wish to thank for making this book a reality. The phrase "It takes a village" could not be more apt in this situation. My earliest thoughts of writing this tome were to share my many years of experience in creating meaningful and beautiful spaces. This did not happen in a solitary bubble.

First and foremost, I want to thank my design partner and best friend, Beau Stinnette. I couldn't do this job without him, and, more importantly, I wouldn't want to. He makes every day more creative, fulfilling, and filled with laughter . . . and, oftentimes, makes it tolerable.

To David Graff, my friend and agent. Without him, this book would not have happened at all.

To my parents, Ned and Frances Foley, who gave me the love of the world and the education to apply those experiences. I love them both infinitely.

To my sister, Mary, and her husband, Stephen, for their unwavering support and for allowing me to experiment with their homes and learning to trust in the vision.

To James Swan, whose good taste and brilliance helped me to focus my writing and create the very first draft of this book.

To Michelle and Richard Lyntton, my friends, my confidantes, and my travel companions. They have given me many years of loving friendship, noteworthy advice, and endless laughter.

To my new friends at Schiffer Publishing, I could not ask for a better or more enthusiastic publisher than Pete Schiffer or a more professional and caring editor than Ann Charles. You guys really make me look good!

To Thom Filicia and Shayla Copas for being inspirations, designers I can aspire to be, and, more importantly, friends.

To the many, many people in my life who have contributed to this book in ways they know or may not be aware of. Josh O'Malley; Christy Pennington; Jimmy Webster Jr.; Sharon Davis; Kristy Hopper; Michael Bauer; Mark, Jason, Julie, and Jessica Philips; Kim Pettigrew; Georgina Weddell; Larry and Sheree Zaslavsky; Steve and Joan Delott; Steve Brown; Mike and Steph Radkay; and to anyone I may have inadvertently left out—it is not due to a lack of gratitude but simply age!

ABOUT THE AUTHOR

Dann Foley is the founder and a principal of Foley & Stinnette Interior Design located in Palm Springs, California. He is renowned designer with projects across North America, Europe, and Asia. His many honors include awards for both interior design and product design. Dann is a speaker, writer, and author on all things design and lifestyle. He is a traditionalist at heart with a style that cannot be defined narrowly. He is known for giving clients personalized interiors, layered in history, with a modern sensibility.

Dann has been featured in many design magazines and designer showhouses. His design style and larger-than-life, approachable personality have been featured on TV shows such as *American Dream Builders* on NBC and *The Real L Word* on Showtime. He is a regular speaker and panelist at the major home shows across the US, where his experience and sense of humor have made him a go-to designers' designer.

His eponymous Dann Foley Lifestyle brand recently debuted the largest single-product launch ever by a licensed designer. Dann's lines are known for their "designer style" that is accessible and affordable. His award-winning designs can be seen and purchased through designers and from retailers across the country as well as at product shows around the globe.

Dann spends his free time at home in Palm Springs, California, as well as traveling regularly to Europe and Asia in search of inspiration for both his designs and his products. Dann is a wanderer at heart, with a love of history, people, and cultures. Dann can be found @DesignerDann on Instagram, Facebook, Twitter, Pinterest, and HOUZZ and at www.foleystinnette.com.